JEWISH PRIDE

JEWISH PRIDE

101 Reasons to Be Proud You're Jewish

MICHAEL SHAPIRO

A BIRCH LANE PRESS BOOK
Published by Carol Publishing Group

A Birch Lane Press Book
Published by Carol Publishing Group
Birch Lane Press is a registered trademark of Carol Communications, Inc.

Editorial, sales and distribution, rights and permissions inquiries should be addressed to Carol Publishing Group, 120 Enterprise Avenue, Secaucus, N.J. 07094

In Canada: Canadian Manda Group, One Atlantic Avenue, Suite 105, Toronto, Ontario M6K 3E7

Carol Publishing Group books may be purchased in bulk at special discounts for sales promotion, fund-raising, or educational purposes. Special editions can be created to specifications. For details, contact Special Sales Department, Carol Publishing Group, 120 Enterprise Avenue, Secaucus, N.J. 07094.

Manufactured in the United States of America
10 9 8 7 6 5 4 3 2 1

Library of Congress Cataloging-in-Publication Data

Shapiro, Michael, 1951–
    Jewish pride : 101 reasons to be proud you're Jewish / Michael
  Shapiro.
        p.   cm.
    "A Birch Lane Press book."
    ISBN 1-55972-393-9 (hc)
    1. Judaism—Miscellanea.   2. Jews—Civilization—Miscellanea.
  I. Title.
  BM51.S53   1997
  296—dc21   97-15827
                                                              CIP
                                                              r97

To Benjamin, Gregory, and Nathaniel
Andrew and Daniel
Ariel and C.K.

With pride

Contents

Introduction

Jews should be proud of their heritage.

But often they are not.

Many Jews, especially in America, want to be like everyone else. Better to be citizens of their country, participants in their nation's great social experiment, and invisible to all who would look too closely than to be obviously Jewish. And what would be obviously Jewish? Beards, wigs, black suits, yarmulkes, thick accents, and big noses? Isn't it safer to shave, wear shorts, sport a baseball cap, curse like an options trader, and go to the plastic surgeon? What's so wrong about fitting in?

Of course, how you look does not necessarily define what you are. But other people may think you are as you appear to be, and some would say it is better and safer to hide behind the same façade as other people: not only in dress, but also in taste and in choice of lifestyle.

Yet Jews should be proud of their heritage and know the reasons why their background is so special.

Too often they are ignorant of their ancestry or they are too frightened or lackadaisical about what is important for their spiritual well-being and for the best interests of others.

Judaism is more than religion. It encompasses a unique, but varied contribution to world history and civilization. Jews should be proud of what their predecessors accomplished, often against the most difficult odds. But pride in their accomplishments is not enough. Hollow boasting is no substitute for understanding the meanings of the wonderful tenets of Jewish thought. Being Jewish does not only mean having an obedient relationship with God. Jewish pride in its best sense connotes a knowledge of Judaism's directive to its people to choose wisely, and in the choosing to benefit not just themselves but all of humanity.

Jews can be proud of themselves only if they know who they are. The quest to know oneself often starts with learning about one's roots. Only through understanding of how Jews created Judaism and Judaism molded the Jewish people can the Chosen People find the sacred path—and be proud of their past in their search for themselves.

PART I

RELIGION

1

Bar/Bat Mitzvah

The bar/bat mitzvah is popularly translated as "son/daughter of the commandments." A recent practice, not more than one hundred years old in the form known today, the bar/bat mitzvah ceremony is conducted differently by the various branches of Judaism. Many Orthodox Jews still reject allowing women of any age to approach and read from the Torah. Reform and Progressive Jews do not even differentiate between girls and boys in celebrations of their coming-of-age ceremonies.

But the basics of the ritual are the same for most Jews—saying prayers with phylacteries, or tefillin, and being called by fellow congregants to read before them from the Torah, or the Law.

Whether the girl is twelve years old and a day or the boy just thirteen, Jewish tradition requires them to acknowledge that they are now cognizant of their acts, that they are now *responsible*; and in their responsibility as human beings can make choices and participate in a quorum (minyan) of their equals, recounting in prayer the paths of behavior of their people through the centuries.

2

Candle Lighting

Jews light candles to usher in and bid farewell to the Sabbath, mourn their dead, accompany young couples to the chuppah at their wedding, and celebrate the miracle of Hanukkah. They light them to remember, to observe, and to keep the brilliance of faith eternal.

Jewish women are urged to light the Sabbath candles every Friday night. Tradition has it that two candles are lit because the Torah lists the Ten Commandments twice (in Exodus and Deuteronomy).

"Remember the Sabbath day to keep it holy." (Exod. 20:8)

"Observe the Sabbath day to keep it holy." (Deut. 5:12)

The Sabbath candles bid Jews to *remember* and *observe*. Jews must remember to take affirmative actions on the holiest day of the week. They must also observe to not do anything that might violate the Shabbat (Sabbath). By lighting the two candles, Jewish women instruct their families to remember the positive and negative aspects of true observance.

So it is when Jews say farewell to the Sabbath "bride" at the twilight service of Havdalah, or "separation." But when they separate themselves from Shabbat, Jews make sure the wicks of the two candles are intertwined—since He "who creates the lights of the fire" refers to a fire that is not singular.

Candlelight is also viewed as a symbol of man's soul. Jews remember their dead relatives with Yahrzeit candles: When a beloved person dies, by lighting these votive-like jars throughout the seven days of mourning (the *shivah*), on each yearly anniversary of the death, and when memorial prayers (*yizkor*) are said in synagogue.

At some Orthodox weddings, parents walk down the aisle with candles, lighting their childrens' way to a marriage brightened by the glow of love and worship.

The most dramatic and some would say most powerful use of candles by Jews is in the candelabrum known as the menorah. Consisting of seven branches, the menorah is one of the two principal symbols of Judaism (the other is, of course, the Star of David). Today, the menorah is viewed as an emblem of pride (despite its desecration in the Arch of Titus in Rome, which celebrated the Empire's destruction of Jerusalem in 70 C.E.). As the centerpiece of the official symbol of the State of Israel, the menorah proclaims the return from exile to freedom.

The concept of the menorah originated with the directive given to

Moses by God in Exodus, "You shall make a candelabrum of pure gold. . . . Its base and its shaft, its branches, its bowls, its knops, and its flowers, shall be of one piece. Six branches shall come out of its sides; three branches out of either side." (Exod. 25:31–38)

The Hanukkah lamp, or *hanukkiyyah*, which adds an eighth branch to the menorah, is but another example of the use of light to remember and observe.

Jews light candles to bring light into the world.

3

Circumcision

"This is my Covenant which you shall keep, between me and you and your progeny after you; every male child among you shall be circumcised." (Gen. 17:10)

For Jews, the covenant of circumcision, or "Brit Milah," represents their special relationship with God. This covenant, which dates back to Abraham, has been known to the world ever since as the defining symbol of Jewry. During the Holocaust, the Germans often identified Jewish men for extinction by examining them to see if they were circumcised. And during the declining years of the Soviet Union, it was a sign of pride for adult Jewish men who had been forbidden a brit at birth by the Communists (also forbidden by the Syrian Greeks during the time of the Maccabees and later by the Romans under Hadrian) to undergo the ritual during their manhood. Indeed, the Bible relates that Abraham was ninety-nine years old when he was circumcised (Ishmael was thirteen)! (Gen. 17:24–25)

Circumcisions are traditionally performed eight days after birth, at which time the infant is given his Hebrew name. The main participants during the circumcision other than the child and his father are the circumciser, or *mohel* (who is sometimes, but not necessarily, a rabbi), and the *sandek* who holds the child during the ritual (often named the godfather). Other people at the ceremony, especially among Ashkenazic Jews, are often asked to perform additional tasks such as carrying the baby to the brit.

The blessings recited at the circumcision underline the meaning of the ceremony. The mohel and the child's father recite blessings reminding all attending that God "has sanctified us with His commandments and commanded us to bring him into the covenant of our father Abraham." Prayers are chanted expressing the wish that as the baby has entered the covenant, so may he study Torah, wed, and *do good deeds*.

4

Covenant

A covenant, or "brit," is an agreement between two different sides.

It is the central mechanism of Jewish thought.

The Bible is full of covenants. The most famous, of course, is the covenant made by Moses at Mt. Sinai, which is usually viewed as an expansion of Abraham's covenants with God.

The first of the two covenants is commonly referred to as the covenant between the pieces (Gen. 15:7–21). Abram (not yet Abraham) asks for confirmation that he will inherit the Land of Canaan. He is instructed to cut a number of animals in half and to arrange their pieces next to each other. God then tells Abram that his offspring (later confirmed through the line started by Isaac) will have the land between "the river of Egypt and the great river Euphrates," but not before they suffer a long exile. Apparently, cutting up animals was a way in ancient times to sanctify an agreement (and a warning to either side that they might end up like the animals if the contract was ever broken!).

The second covenant is that of circumcision, when Abram becomes Abraham, and God promises that "I will maintain my Covenant between me and you, and your descendants to come as an everlasting Covenant through the ages, to be God to you and to your descendants to come." (Gen. 17:7)

Later, after the Exodus from Egypt, God reveals His law at Mt. Sinai to the Jewish people. The Ten Commandments, of course, form the centerpiece of the Sinaitic revelation. It is not a revelation that is made only to Moses; it is a public revelation meant to be experienced by *all* people. This divine manifestation, or "theophany," is not the work of great thinkers over centuries or the ruling of a great king. It is not a scholarly text. Jewish experience mandates that it is wholly and inseparably the word of God. And the Ten Commandments, unlike other ancient codes (like that of Hammurabi), are about morality, not property, life, or death.

Despite occasional lapses during the thousands of years since, the Jewish people have remained bound to this third covenant made in the wilderness of Sinai. For out of God's revelation to all their ears and hearts came the essence of civilization—morality and ethics founded not in secular law but in religious belief.

5

Festivals

To Jews, each of their festivals is a good day (*yom tov*).

The Bible forbids work on seven of these festival days: Rosh Hashanah (the Jewish New Year, 1 Tishri), Yom Kippur (the Day of Atonement, 10 Tishri), Sukkot (the first day of Tabernacles, 15 Tishri), Shemini Atzeret (the eighth day of Solemn Assembly, 22 Tishri), the beginning and the end of Pesach (Passover, 15 and 22 Nisan), and Shavuot (the Festival of Weeks, also known as the Festival of the Giving of Our Torah and the Festival of the First Fruits, 6–7 Sivan).

Yom Kippur is the only fast day among the festivals. On most of the other festival days the celebrations are marked with special foods including, but certainly not limited to, honey and apples, potato pancakes (latkes), round challah loaves, honey cakes, kreplach (the Jewish equivalent of the Chinese wonton), three-sided poppyseed buns ("hamantashen," named for Haman, the villain of Purim), and unleavened bread (matzo).

There are additional festivals, some added recently, on which work is permitted, but certain aspects of remembrance are mandated. These include Purim; Hanukkah; Tu bi-Shevat (the New Year for trees); Purim Katan (the so-called Lesser Purim, which is celebrated in leap years on the fourteenth or fifteenth [in Jerusalem] day of Adar); the "Second" Passover (observed on 14 Iyar by those unable to participate in the Passover held one month earlier); Lag ba-Omer (the thirty-third day of the *omer*, or "sheaf," held on 18 Iyar, a period of restriction and remembrance, often called the Scholars' Festival in memory of the students of Rabbi Akiba who were killed during the Bar Kokhba rebellion [132–135 C.E.]); and Hamishah Asar be-Av (the fifteenth day of Av, an ancient festive holiday from the days of the Second Temple, when young women would dress all in white and dance in vineyards before their beaux); Yom ha-Atsma-ut (Israel's Independence Day, 5 Iyar); and Yom Yerushalayim (Jerusalem Day, 28 Iyar).

Festivals are dates in the year when Jews are reminded of the essentials of their faith.

6

The High Holy Days

Rosh Hashanah (the Jewish New Year) and Yom Kippur (the Day of Atonement) are the most sacred days in the Jewish calendar.

Rosh Hashanah begins on the first day of Tishri, the first day of the Hebrew New Year. Yom Kippur occurs on the tenth day of Tishri and is the culmination of what are called the Ten Days of Repentance.

Jews should be proud of how they start their calendar each year. Rather than partying wildly (as in many other cultures), Jews look into themselves. The New Year is a time of introspection and meditation. Not only are Jews to be judged by God, they must judge themselves. Before each of them is the image of every Jewish man and woman appearing before the throne of God sitting in a judgment to be entered on Rosh Hashanah and sealed on Yom Kippur. The rabbis taught that God kept three great ledgers open in Heaven: the Book of Life for the righteous, the Book of Death for the horridly evil, and a third book for most of the rest of us. During the Days of Awe between Rosh Hashanah and Yom Kippur, a person's fate is set.

On Rosh Hashanah, Jews greet each other with the hope that each "may be inscribed for a good year." At home, celebratory meals reflect the spiritual purposes of the holiday. After a short prayer, a piece of apple is dipped in honey, accompanied with the optimistic saying that hopefully one's new year will be as sweet. Round challah loaves are eaten with the wish that a "good round year" will follow.

With the blast of a ram's horn, or "shofar," sounding the call of the faithful to God and the tearing up of Satan, erasing the evil that has multiplied during the prior year, Rosh Hashanah marks the anniversary of man's creation, a new beginning when through repentance, prayer, and charity humanity can be reborn.

The Day of Atonement is the Sabbath of all Sabbaths (but despite its special holiness is not more important than each week's Sabbath!).

Jews are asked not only to fast for twenty-five hours on Yom Kippur, but to repent, to confess their sins (the *vidui*), to ask for God's forgiveness, and to make their peace with God as well. Atoning for one's sins against God on Yom Kippur is no relief, however, from sins committed against other people. Jews are urged to settle up with those they have hurt before Yom Kippur so as to better approach the Day of Atonement with a clear mind and heart.

The chanting of Kol Nidre, or "all vows," before the onset of Yom Kippur is the most moving and melodically beautiful moment in the Jewish year. The cantor, sometimes aided by two other congregants, annuls the vows of all attending. But the vows that are annulled are only those between people and God. Every person is still held accountable for what he or she has done to or said about others.

On Yom Kippur the dead are remembered in a memorial service called *yizkor* (also observed on three other occasions—the last days of Passover, Shavuot, and Shemini Atzeret). The message implied by the yizkor service is that the beloved departed are best remembered through charity and the doing of good deeds.

When the Day of Atonement concludes (the *ne'ilah* service), Jews not only beg God to be written into the Book of Life, but they restate seven times that "The Lord Is God; The Lord Is One" (the *Shema*), pledging to one another to spend the *coming* year in Jerusalem.

7

Kiddush

Kiddush means "sanctification."

The Kiddush is an ancient prayer said while holding a cup or goblet of wine, often, but not always, before a meal. The Kiddush is meant to be said at home and in the synagogue at the end of Friday night and other services and at public occasions such as festive meals. The table set with food to be consumed is not to be, therefore, just a repast but a pulpit, a blessing.

The Kiddush is not just a prayer over wine. It is traditionally in two parts, a blessing over wine and for the day. Those making the Kiddush stand, share the wine after the blessing, and often wash their hands before saying an additional blessing over the bread to be eaten at the meal.

For Jews, to recite the Kiddush is to bless their home, their very existence, and to differentiate themselves from eating like animals, from simply satisfying their hunger for food. Saying the Kiddush reminds Jews to thank God for the gift of Shabbat and the sanctity of His commandments. In this one prayer they remember the Creation and the Exodus from Egypt, recounting indeed, the very essence of Judaism.

8

Kippah (Yarmulke)

A Jewish male wears a skullcap (called "kippah" in Hebrew and "yarmulke" in Yiddish) to show his reverence for God.

Jewish law does not require their use. Even the most sacred prayer can be uttered without a head covering. However, it has been established custom since the days of the composition of the Talmud that men and boys cover their heads, especially when praying and sometimes during meals. Many Orthodox Jewish men are proud to cover their heads at all times, while the custom is observed by Conservative Jews mostly in the synagogue and during private prayer and study, and by those in the Reform movement even less regularly.

All Jews, however, recognize the transcendent symbolism of the kippah. Mankind is beneath God. The skullcap reminds Jews of the Almighty's dominance over their lives. It is not just a sign of submission, but also a proud acknowledgment to themselves and to the world of a loving obedience.

Some guess that the Yiddish term *yarmulke* is derived from an Aramaic phrase signifying an awe of God. And many view the wearing of one as a continual affirmation of faith. Since the early 1700s, the pious have identified with its expressive intent as both an outward- and an inner-directed affirmation of devotion.

There were times in Jewish history when Gentile governments insisted that Jews wear hats (sometime pointed ones, as in Germany) to separate them visually from an oppressive majority. Yet since the time the Nazis sought to knock all the yarmulkes off of European Jewry, contemporary Jews have often worn their *kippot* as emblems of pride in and loyalty to Judaism. Finely knit kippot, sometimes handmade by wives and girlfriends, adorn the heads of many modern Jews. The wearing of the skullcap is the most obvious mark of Jewish pride.

9

Kosher

One could question why Jews should be proud of their strict dietary laws. Most other peoples can enjoy eating relatively anything. A trip to the beach can be topped with a fresh lobster roll, a Saturday morning out with the kids crowned with a Big Mac for lunch, or the weekend concluded with a large helping of Chinese food (such as pork fried rice and spare ribs!).

Yet the Torah, rabbinic law, and custom restrain Jews from mixing meat and milk at the same meal, from eating shellfish, pork, insects of any kind (except a few varieties of locusts!), or any animal not slaughtered pursuant to approved ritual. "You will not seethe a kid in its mother's milk." (Exod. 23:19, 34:26; Deut. 14:21) The rules concerning kashrut (translated as "fitness"), are numerous and demand careful attention in their observance. These regulations have caused friction among religious and secular Jews. Indeed, many Reform Jews view them as cumbersome and outdated, while there are some Orthodox

Jews who insist on only their definition of what is *glatt*, or strictly kosher.

The popular assumption that the determination of what is fit to eat came from an ancient but enlightened understanding of hygiene and dietetics is misconceived. During the Middle Ages, the great philosopher and commentator Maimonides asserted that observing kashrut protected us from unwholesome food and, in his almost Aristotelian view, instructed in how our appetites could be controlled. "Keeping" kosher has also been viewed by some as indicating a caring way of life because of the requirement that animals be slaughtered rapidly without causing them any pain. Kashrut laws dictate that blood and carnivorous animals cannot be consumed. Only plant-eating creatures, mammals that have split hooves *and* chew their cud, and fish with fins and scales can be eaten (sorry, no pigs or shrimp!).

Jews observe their dietary laws for no other reason than that the Torah tells them to. There is no explanation given in the law. No reasons, no rational or scientific explanations, just faith. You believe it or you do not.

But, again, what is there to be proud of?

Consider the following three laws of kashrut: 1. Birds that have talons to kill their prey may not be eaten. 2. Failure of the *shohet* (slaughterer) to kill an animal with one fast stroke renders it unkosher (his blade must be perfectly sharp). 3. Jews are banned from hunting animals (how many Jewish hunters do you know?).

In the most difficult of times, Jews have preserved the laws of kashrut. The Jewish hatred of spilling blood is most likely derived from their dietary restrictions against consuming it—kashrut, therefore, as one of the great civilizing forces. For to observe kashrut is equated in the Torah with a state of holiness (Lev. 11:44–45).

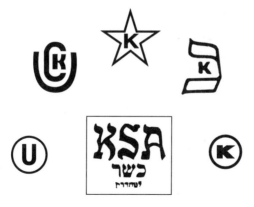

10

Matzo

"This is the bread of affliction that our ancestors ate in the Land of Egypt."

The Haggadah, the Passover text read twice every year, reminds Jews that at each seder an olive weight's worth of matzo must be eaten. Jews are urged not to forget that they were once slaves to Pharaoh. Jewish people eat matzo to commemorate their rapid flight from their Egyptian oppressors. The dough on Israelite backs baked (but did not rise!) in the brutally hot sun during their meandering path across the desert.

Jewish law contains special rules concerning the baking of matzo. Flour derived from one of five grains is mixed with water and baked (for not more than eighteen minutes!) before the dough rises. If there is any fermentation, then the bread is not unleavened and is considered to be *chametz*, or unfit to be eaten during Passover.

In addition to its long association with the Passover holiday, matzo was also utilized in the ancient Temple in Jerusalem as a sacred part of altar ceremonies and ritual meals (Lev. 2:4–5).

Jews differ on which varieties of matzo (wheat, egg, chocolate!) can be consumed during Passover. Some will only eat matzo that has been made from grain carefully kept from any contact with water—until right before baking. This so-called *shmura*, or "guarded," matzo is customarily handmade and, perhaps due to its pure derivation, is usually the most authentic and, some would rave, tastiest matzo. Ashkenazic tradition permits the consumption of egg matzo during Passover only by children, the elderly, and those suffering from illness.

Despite the rich history and symbolic meaning of matzo, anti-Semites, ranging from those in Lincoln, England, in the thirteenth century to those in czarist Kiev in the early twentieth, created the "blood libel," using the image of Jews baking unleavened bread made with the blood of Christian children to foment riots, pogroms, and the slaughter of Jewish innocents.

Whether the symbol of matzo is used by Jews to remember their ancient slavery or by bigots who seek to subjugate or destroy them, it remains a potent reminder that liberty is not so easily won or sustained. There are forces throughout history that would deny not only Jewry, but all people, the sanctity of what is surely their natural right—their freedom.

The bread of affliction is therefore an emblem of courage for everyone (not only Jews), of release from pain and oppression. Few foods carry such historical weight and symbolic power.

11

Messiah

Jews have waited so long for the Messiah. Messianism, or the belief in an anointed one, or redeemer, dates back to ancient times during the Babylonian captivity. The yearning for the Messiah is expressed throughout the Bible and in traditional Jewish prayers.

The concept of the Messiah has developed in Jewish history from the hope for a glorious age ruled by a descendant of King David to mystical and often frightening images of the end of the world, Armageddon, resurrection of the dead, and final judgment.

Persecution and suffering have led Jews on several occasions to follow false messiahs. The catastrophe of the rebellion in 135 C.E., when Bar Kokhba was crowned messiah by Rabbi Akiba (leading to the fall of ancient Judea, the massacre of hundreds of thousands, and dispersion into the Roman Empire) and the antics of Sabbatai Tzvi in the Balkans during the seventeenth century both followed periods of immense torment and subjugation.

In modern times the establishment of settlements in what was shortly to become the State of Israel triggered the hope in some (including Rav Kook, the first Ashkenazic chief rabbi of Palestine) that a messianic age was approaching. Indeed, it has been documented that during the Holocaust, many Jews when faced with their deaths sang out their belief, in the Hebrew words of Maimonides, *ani maamin,* that the days of the Messiah were near!

Each branch of Judaism places its own emphasis on what the Messiah will bring to our earthly life. Many Orthodox Jews expect that the Temple in Jerusalem will be rebuilt, ritual sacrifices will be reinstituted, all those exiled during the Diaspora will be gathered back into Zion, and every religious requirement of Jewish law will be fulfilled. Conservative tradition is not far behind, but with more emphasis on the establishment of permanent peace in the world with all malevolence vanquished and sickness vanished. The Reform movement has turned the image of the Messiah to a more modern use. For Reform Jews there is no individual or personal messiah. Rather, messianic symbolism is used to push us toward intellectual and spiritual improvement. The Reconstructionist movement repudiates the idea of a messiah completely.

Of course, the Jewish concept of the Messiah led to the most famous messianic figure in history, Jesus of Nazareth. There are some Jews whose prejudice would lead them to say that this is not something to be proud of. Certainly the hatred of the Jews by generations of people who defined themselves as Christians led to massacres during the Crusades, the Spanish Inquisition, the Chmielnicki revolt, Czarist pogroms, and the Shoah. Although there is much common ground between the two faiths, the religious ties between Judaism and Christianity come unwound when faced with the choice of whether to accept or reject Jesus as the Messiah. Clearly this is not something Jews and Christians can ever agree on.

Jews can, however, find much pride in their role in the Judeo-Christian ethic that forms the basis of our civilization.

Jews can also be proud when thinking of the effect the idea of the Messiah had on Zionism. Zionists did not wait for the Messiah to come. After the Hitler years, the messianic urge was secularized, returning via the most productive reaction in Jewish history, the creation of the State of Israel.

12

Mezuzah

"And you shall write them upon the doorposts of your house and upon your gates. . . ." (Deut. 6:9, 11:20)

Jews are required by the Torah to affix a mezuzah to all the doorposts in their homes (except those leading to bathrooms or small storage rooms). In Israel, mezuzahs must be attached immediately upon moving in; elsewhere Jews are required to have mezuzahs in place not later than thirty days after establishing a home.

Although *mezuzah* is the Hebrew word for doorpost, it has become known as the name for the scroll of parchment upon which specific passages from the Bible are handwritten by a scribe. The parchment *must* be derived from a clean animal. The biblical text *must* conform to ancient rules of calligraphy. The mezuzah *must* be nailed into the upper right side of the doorpost about a hand's length down from the top. The mezuzah *must* (according to Ashkenazic tradition) be placed at a forty-five-degree angle. The mezuzah scroll *must* contain the words of the beginning of the Shema, or the call to the Jewish people that "the

Lord Is One." In addition, the doorway upon which the mezuzah is affixed *must* meet certain measurement requirements.

Must, not may.

The mezuzah is customarily kissed by the observant, who touch it as they enter or leave a house or a room and bring the Biblical message to their lips. This custom symbolizes that they are enlightened of its contents. Others believe that upon blessing the house with the gesture of putting up the mezuzah, evil is prevented from entering one's dwelling place. It is certainly a gesture of peace and devotion. Kiss the mezuzah and you simply know how to act everywhere, whether it be at home or in the world.

Why then do so many forget its message?

Few other peoples require this kind of piety. Certainly other religions demand the devoted bow to altars in houses of worship. Some other cultures bring religion into the home with icons or statuary. Jews are required by the Torah to kiss the Word of God (the acronym of one of God's names made up of the Hebrew letters *shin*, *daled*, and *yod* inscribed on the outside of the scroll) as they enter and leave, not their place of business or worship, but rather their homes, where they sleep, raise their families, and enjoy life. Jews are reminded that holiness is to be found and sought in all places.

All they need to do is look at the doorposts of their houses to remember.

13

Midrash

Jews seem never to be content to accept anything at face value. It is almost conventional among Jewish people that they question everything. The method used by rabbis through the centuries to explain the Scriptures and to clarify Jewish law is called *Midrash* in Hebrew. Midrash means "exposition."

Inquiry, study, investigation, preaching, seeking God's law, going beneath the words found in holy scrolls, and using parables, tales, and legends to explicate are the driving forces of Midrash. Midrash also refers to a huge body of literature that developed out of its explanatory techniques. Midrash Aggadah, Midrash Ha-Gadol (the so-called "Great" Midrash), Midrash Halakhah, Midrash Proverbs, Midrash Samuel, Midrash Tadshe, Midrash Tanhuma, Midrash Tehillim, and Midrash Va-Yissa'u are the titles of some of these huge categories or compendiums of Midrashic literature. Whether explaining the law through tales, legal exegesis, proverbs, psalm telling, or the stories of Biblical heroes such as Jacob, Midrash is a process that utilizes literary methods of analysis.

The midrashic method is called *derash* and is literally a means of searching out the truth. An almost Hellenic use of logic is applied in analyzing sacred language. Comparable phrases from other sources are set against the words being analyzed, ideas are inferred from textual hints, and sometimes wild leaps of fancy are used to explain puzzling Biblical phrases. Metaphor and allegory are used to explain the unexplained.

From Midrash comes what is known in Christian churches as the "homily." The Muslims also consulted midrashic sources for many of the biblical legends found in the Koran.

Midrash asks eternal questions. That it supplies so many answers is its miracle.

14

Mishnah

Perhaps the bravest act an oppressed people can make—even more than armed rebellion—is that of quiet remembrance through the recording of its essential lessons.

The codification of the oral law of the Jewish people, called the Mishnah, was carried out from 200 to 220 C.E. under the supervision of Rabbi Judah Ha-Nasi (translated variously as Judah the Prince or Judah the Patriarch). Two disastrous rebellions against Roman domination in 70 and 135 C.E. had resulted in the deaths of over one million Jews and the dispersion of the remnants into the Roman Empire. The bulk of Jewish law not set forth in the Torah had been passed down by word of mouth by great teachers to generations of students. Most of the teachers had perished in the Roman wars. The favored practice of the speaking of the Law, keeping the student physically close to the teacher, was no longer possible. Judah's decision to write it all down (conflicting versions and all) was a courageous and successful attempt at preserving the soul of ancient Judaism.

Mishnah means "teaching" or "instruction." Unlike the Five Books of Moses that comprise the Torah and tell what is in essence Biblical history, the Mishnah is a code, a place to look up laws and regulated practices. For example, to learn Jewish rules concerning marriage, one would refer to the order or section of the Mishnah called Women (*Nashim*). The other five orders (*sedarim*) of the Mishnah cover agriculture, civil and criminal law, sacrifices, ritual purity, and festivals. These orders are further subdivided into sixty-three tractates (*masekhot*).

What would appear as organized, however, is often a jumble since related subjects and arguments between rival commentators work their way under headings to which they often have no relation. What has been dubbed "stream of consciousness" by some modern authorities gives the Mishnah its human quality and timeless appeal.

It is upon the storehouse of rules found in the Mishnah that the commentaries of the Talmud (and those of Maimonides and others) were based.

In a time of horror and death, the apparent final destruction of the Jewish homeland, and never-ending slavery, the decision was made to preserve a heritage in writing so that no one could ever forget its truth.

15

Monotheism

שְׁמַע יִשְׂרָאֵל: יְיָ אֱלֹהֵינוּ, יְיָ אֶחָד!

Hear, O Israel: the Lord is our God, the Lord is One!

—Deut. 6:4–9; Deut. 11:13–21; Num. 15:37–41

The Jewish belief in one God changed the world. It is expressed in the Shema, a Biblical verse that Jews are commanded to read twice a day, when they lie down and rise up. The Shema relates, in the simplest expression, that God exists, has a unique relationship with all Jewish people, and is singular and unified.

Although the Jewish concept of divinity has been viewed by some modern commentators as conservative, it was revolutionary when first conceived and a great spiritual advance for all people. Ancient religions were typically dominated by pantheons of gods who represented the endless variety and often random violence of earthly life.

Jewish monotheism added reason and morality to religious belief. To believe in one God is a rationalization and a step of faith. All things in the universe come from one source intimately involved in all elements of their existence. The "Jewish God" is everywhere and in everyone. Since God is in all things, murdering another destroys the whole world, and saving a life redeems all. If one believes in one God, then the whole world is unified, for humanity is one with the Lord.

The idea of one God is proof to generations that there is a purpose to life. Not only is monotheism the essence of Judaic thought (and its descendant religions, Christianity and Islam), belief in one God is the fundamental basis for all civilization.

16

Prayer

Jews should be proud of *tefillah*, or the way they pray.

Judaism espouses a view that mankind has a personal relationship with God. As man was created in God's image, people have a personal connection with their Creator.

Yet the rabbis remind us that we do not pray just to get God's forgiveness or to give repeated praise to the Lord. The word *tefillah* is derived from the Hebrew for "to think, to intervene, to judge one's own being, to look inward, not just out to the Heavens where one can have no responsibility."

By helping us to become more aware of ourselves, prayer improves our affinity with all that is holy in ourselves.

Some Jews need help in making their prayer devout. *Davening*, or swaying while praying, has become a sign of piety. Moving one's body to the rhythm of the syllables of devoted prayer often adds a physical ecstasy when divining the mysteries of the liturgy.

Jews face East toward Jerusalem when they pray (a custom copied by the early Christians and by all Muslims, who face toward Mecca), for Jews have been justly proud of their origins and are directed by law and tradition to face toward the capital of their country and the original site of the Holy of Holies.

17

Prophecy

The gift of prophecy is claimed by many cultures. For example, the oracle at Delphi was a visionary source for the ancient Greeks. What will come next? When will the crops grow? Is it safe to venture forth onto the sea? All these are just a sampling of the questions asked of seers who gazed into an unknowable and mysterious future.

Yet, Jewish prophecy and the prophets who shared their revelations with the people were markedly different in approach and result from those in other societies. Jewish prophets claimed an intimacy with the word of God and a moral view of life that they sought to impose on their fellow Jews. Religion for the Jewish prophet was not empty ritual. The prophets were obsessed—God filled—with the substance of Jewish law. Its ceremonies were only a means to express the true sources of Judaism.

Jewish prophets arose from all walks of life. Whether aristocrat, priest, farmer, or patriarch, the prophet was one with the people even when he was demanding that they cease erring from God's laws.

These prophets seemed to know before the common folk when disaster would strike next. Disaster, they often asserted, followed because the people had been sinful. Godliness resulted in happiness, sin in catastrophe. The formation of the Jewish people and of the concept of Judaism as not just a religion but also a civilizing force came out of the fervor of prophets.

The intuitions of Jewish prophets, often expressed in screaming, symbolic acts, or musical chant, molded the development of oral Jewish law. Before the writing down of the Law in Torah, Mishnah, and Talmud, the prophets acted as the guiding power in shaping the Jewish moral universe.

Jews can be justly proud of the power and responsibility of Jewish prophecy. The Jewish prophets used their intuition for the betterment of the world, not to simply predict, like a genie, what would come next.

18

Psalms

Hymns of praise, lamentations, expressions of hope, extravagant phrases, declamations of faith—all are descriptive of the power and majesty of the psalms.

Many people are surprised to learn that the Book of Psalms is a major and highly expressive section of the Bible. Indeed, a separate psalter is available to worshippers at the Western Wall in Jerusalem along with a *siddur*, or prayer book. Psalms have not only been utilized to highly symbolic effect in Jewish liturgy, but they play an equivalent role in Christian services, particularly those of Protestant denominations. Psalms provide Jewish prayer with both humanity and awe of God.

Although many psalms are attributed to King David and some to King Solomon and others, historians place their composition hundreds of years later in the period after the Jews' ancient exile in Babylon. The inclusion of psalm verses in the liturgy evolved out of their usage in the Second Temple in Judea before its destruction by the Romans in

70 C.E. It is thought that some of the psalms were sung by pilgrims as they ascended the steps of the Temple (thus the title "Song of Ascents"), or sung by the priests with instrumental accompaniment (a ritual long forgotten). Sometimes psalms entered the liturgy whole, other times in pieces, an incorporation into Jewish prayer that ended in the late Middle Ages. Whether tied to the celebration of particular festivals, like Hanukkah, or cataloged in essential lists required for daily recitation, the psalms have given an emotional thrust to Jewish worship.

Many of the one hundred fifty psalms contained in the Bible are creative masterworks, truly some of the greatest poems ever written. People's feelings about life and their belief in God are profoundly set forth with a passion and clarity not found in other ancient literature. How to feel hope, the feeling of being abject before God's immeasurable force, recognizing the smallness of human endeavor and the over-whelming righteousness of divine intervention: These are just some of the subjects of these personal yet public psalms. The psalms tell us that there is no shame in feeling shame and no despair incapable of being conquered.

The psalms are an ancient recital of truth. Declaring the message of God in song and proclamation brings us hope over misery and respite after pain.

19

Rabbi

Rabbi means "teacher" or "master."

The term *rabbi* is ancient, dating back at least to the first century C.E. Indeed, in some Christian literature and folklore, Jesus of Nazareth is called a rabbi. Originally the term was used to show respect. Later it became known as a way of identifying those who were experts in and taught others Jewish law.

Old tradition holds that rabbis were created by the "laying of hands" (in Hebrew, *semikhat yadayim*). Moses was the first such master, passing the tradition onto Joshua's shoulders. Later, after the exile, or Diaspora, had broken the chain created by such masters, each rabbi had the right to make someone else a rabbi. Such other person, however, had to be worthy of the title. Worth was judged by that person's character and knowledge of the Torah.

For the past one hundred fifty years, rabbis in the United States have come from rabbinical colleges such as those at Yeshiva University and the Jewish Theological Seminary in New York and Hebrew Union College in New York and Cincinnati. Such rabbinical colleges, sometimes called seminaries, have developed their own core curricula and mandated requirements for granting the honor of rabbi.

The role of the rabbi has changed over the centuries. In ancient times, rabbis were often judges and sometimes members of the Sanhedrin, the Judean legislature. During the many years of exile, and especially among Ashkenazic Jewry, rabbis acted as Talmudic sages, interpreting the law and directing the lives of the common people, often acting as governments-in-exile. The period considered the Dark Ages for most Europeans was an age of renaissance for generations of rabbis of genius who toiled in obscurity, interpreting the sacred word over and over again and keeping their people together.

The activities of the rabbi have altered over time. Jewish needs have differed throughout the world, and so has rabbinic focus. During the days of the British Empire, some English Jews dubbed their rabbis "reverends," expressing a clear desire to blend into a mostly Protestant society. In many American synagogues today, the duties of rabbis are mostly pastoral, not much different from their religious brethren in the churches and cathedrals across the country. Only in ultra-Orthodox communities do rabbis still retain an almost secular authority similar to their medieval forebears.

Yet, Jews should be immensely proud of their form of leader, the rabbi. Other cultures may determine leadership by choosing their strongest and most domineering. Warrior societies have ruled the earth for most of recorded time. Perhaps the failure of Jewish communities to control their destinies in foreign lands was ordained by their leadership structure. They chose not the strongest, but the wisest; not the simplest, but the most complex mind. Their choice was a rabbi, a leader, a master who sought through understanding the divine word how his people should live in an imperfect world.

20

Revelation

Abraham and Moses did not choose to be prophets and leaders of their people. They were chosen by God. Tradition holds that "the god who has no name" revealed himself to them through speech. Revelation is at the core of all Jewish prophecy—every Jew's direct and intimate relationship with God—and in many ways is the basis for all its religious beliefs.

At some point, many believe, having faith in God is similar to taking a leap without looking down. This so-called leap of faith means that God has revealed Himself to one's people and His revelation is acknowledged.

Rabbis believe that God has not revealed himself to the prophets of the Jewish people since the destruction of the First Temple and the deaths of Haggai, Zechariah, and Malachi. Yet over the centuries, thinkers and writers have taken the concept of revelation and adapted it to their own value structures and modes of expression. For example,

Maimonides sought revelation through the application of reason and philosophy, while the poet Judah Halevi reveled in the supernatural presence of God and His loving, enveloping Spirit. More contemporary voices (such as Buber, Kook, Soloveitchik, and Heschel) have variously connected revelation to productive spiritual activity, including Torah study, personally returning to the land of Israel; or how belief impacts our everyday lives. Reform and Reconstructionist Judaism, on the other hand, reject revelation as a supernatural phenomenon.

The concept of God's revelation to the Jews, His seeking out of the Jewish people, not any other people, for unique purpose, has been a harsh burden for Jews. The core of Jewry's role in the world is to relate His revelation to *all* people. God is not just for Jews but is universal, His revelation stirring Christians and Muslims to attend also to a vision of God urging the people to righteousness.

21

Sabbath

And on the seventh day God finished the work which He had been doing, and He rested on the seventh day from all the work which He had done. And God blessed the seventh day and declared it holy, because on it God ceased from all the work of creation which He had done.   —Gen. 2:1–3

Remember the Sabbath day and keep it holy.   —Exod. 20:8

Remember that you were a slave in the land of Egypt and the Lord your God freed you from there with a mighty hand and an out-stretched arm; therefore the Lord your God has commanded you to observe the Sabbath day.   —Deut. 5:12–15

Keep my Sabbaths, for this is a sign between me and you throughout the generations, that you may know that I the Lord have consecrated you . . . a covenant for all time: it shall be a sign for all time between me and the people of Israel. For in six days the Lord made the heaven and earth, and on the seventh day He ceased from work and was refreshed.

—Exod. 31:13–17

Creation, a day of rest, a symbol of the Jewish people's special covenant with God, a remembrance of their rescue from slavery in Egypt—the Sabbath (*Shabbat* in Hebrew) is the holiest day of the Jewish week. The Jewish mystics called Shabbat the Sabbath Queen, adding a feminine, almost procreative urge, to the seventh day of the week.

Yet, the Sabbath, while an emblem of the beginning of all things (one can start anew each week), is also a day marked by regulations. On the Sabbath one is required to avoid work (*melachah*). God rested from creation—so should you. The written law set forth in the Mishnah prohibits thirty-nine major categories of work (such as plowing, washing, weaving, lighting a fire, moving something from one place to another). Anything you can do that could be viewed as work or anything that can be used for work (remember to remove all your sewing needles from your pockets so you do not carry them around!), in short, anything that will change the world from what it is before the Sabbath, is strictly forbidden.

The Sabbath sets the Jews apart from all other peoples but also creates an example for them to follow. In allocating one day a week to rest, to contemplation; in creating an island of tranquility amid a week of struggle, hardship, and "making ends meet;" the home, mind, and spirit become transformed. More than just a change of pace, the Sabbath brings another dimension, some have said an additional "soul," to living. The observance of the Sabbath is one of the most important Jewish contributions to world civilization, the day of rest as an expression of joy and comfort for humanity in God's world.

22

Seder

Seder means "order."

The Seder is the elaborate ritual meal customarily held in Jewish homes on the first two nights of Passover (only one night in Israel). The order of the Seder is proscribed in the Mishnah, its customs having developed largely after the destruction of the Second Temple in Jerusalem during 70 C.E.

The ancient Greek and Roman symposia are probably the only comparable tradition. While the symposium is best learned about by reading Plato, the Seder remains a vital centerpiece of Jewish practice.

Jews are not commonly known to frequent taverns, yet they are required to drink four cups of wine at the Seder. Each drink at the Seder is accompanied by prayer and song, the context of drinking given a resonance and meaning particularly Hebraic.

A ceremony rich in meaning and history, the Seder brings families together for a few hours each year to share the joy and freedom of their households. It was not always so peaceful. The Passover Seder usually coincides with Easter, which was a time historically of great danger to Jews, particularly those in Eastern Europe. Despite the ancient practice of leaving one's front door open throughout the Seder to welcome the Prophet Elijah, frightened Jews often greeted him only briefly, quickly shutting the entries to their homes lest hoodlums notice the consecration of Passover. The alleged ritual slaughter of Gentile children and the use of their blood to make matzos led to persecution often countenanced by the state.

Despite this history, the Seder truly is a miracle of civilization. Before, during, and after the family enjoys a special meal with symbolic foods, a short book is read—the *Haggadah*—and some parts are sung. The Haggadah tells the story of the Israelites' plight in Egypt, their slavery and loss of dignity; their exodus from the Nile to the Promised Land; their wandering in the desert; and, finally, their redemption in the Promised Land. Children are taught that God led their ancestors out of Egypt with "a strong hand and an outstretched arm."

There is no gloating, however, about the drowning of the Egyptians in the Red Sea. Jews remind one another at the Seder that we were once strangers in their land and that Egyptians are also children of God.

The Seder is a remarkably early example in history of compassion and feeling.

23

Shivah

The Jewish way of mourning is, like all things in Jewish life, ordered.

Not that one should not grieve. Jewish tradition requires that one literally tear one's garments when learning of the death of a loved one, especially a parent. Judaism demands that the reality of death be addressed without holding back. Weeping in public, even shrieking among some Sephardic Jews, is hardly frowned on. The pain of losing a dear relative or friend is often more than any of us can bear. Yet the Jewish religion dictates that mourning should not, cannot, must not, continue beyond a certain point. Life, that most precious of all things for all Jews, will proceed. Jews are instructed by the Law not to attend any parties for just under a year after the death of a close relation, to recite the Mourner's Prayer, or Kaddish daily during that period, and to pray for their remembrance at *yizkor* services on Yom Kippur, on Shemini Atzeret (the eighth day of Sukkot), on the last day of Passover, and on Shavuot. These observances are meant not only for the dead. Mostly, they are for those who have survived and must go on.

When Jewish people die, it is required that they be buried as soon as possible; this usually means during the same day, before the coming of night. This is viewed as a gesture of respect for the dead. Open coffins, lengthy, loud, and boisterous wakes, drinking, carousing around the dead, parading about are all viewed by traditional Judaism as improper. The departed are to be cherished, held dear. It is felt this cannot occur amid raucous behavior.

One of the most blessed and enlightened acts anyone can do is to prepare the dead for burial. This is not a job for everyone. Jews have long organized burial societies, groups of men and women whose job it is to purify the deceased according to established ritual and to be sure they are not left alone until interment. After terrorist bombings in Israel, the world has viewed with amazement and respect those humble members of burial societies who search for body parts in trees and strewn across streets, since they must be buried as well.

While every Jew does not have to participate in a burial society, every Jew is required by the Law to observe the one week of *Shivah* after the death of a parent, brother or sister, child, or spouse. Shivah simply means "seven," for the first and most difficult of mourning periods. After the funeral, after the casting of clods of earth on the lowered casket—the parting final, irrevocable—Jews are supposed to remain at home, seated on low stools, receiving visitors, not being left alone, so they can slowly rejoin their community. Guests are cautioned to appreciate the pain of the bereaved, to listen to them, and not to speak out of turn or about anything trivial. The Jewish way of mourning is all about consideration, deference to the loving memory of the life lost, as the rest of us carry on.

עֹשֶׂה שָׁלוֹם בִּמְרוֹמָיו, הוּא יַעֲשֶׂה שָׁלוֹם עָלֵינוּ וְעַל־כָּל־

O·seh sha·lom bi·me·ro·mav, hu ya·a·seh sha·lom a·lei·nu ve·al kol

יִשְׂרָאֵל, וְאִמְרוּ: אָמֵן.

Yis·ra·eil, ve·i·me·ru: a·mein.

24

Shofar

"In the seventh month, on the first day of the month, you will observe a sacred occasion: You will not work at your occupations. You will observe it as a day when the horn is sounded." (Num. 31:1)

The shofar is a musical instrument made out of a ram's horn. During ancient times this kind of trumpet was used to call Israelites to war, to herald the beginning of a jubilee and the Sabbath, and to rejoice in the crowning of kings. Since the establishment of the State of Israel, the swearing in of a new president has been marked by the blowing of the shofar.

Although the shofar was blown every day in the Temple in Jerusalem, its use today is limited to the High Holy Days. Still, it remains a potent symbol. The sounds of wailing notes (*shevarim*), staccato blasts (*teru'ah*), and long held rising tones (*teki'ah*) hold almost primal significance for Jews each new year.

The shofar sounds like no modern instrument. Derived from a ritually acceptable animal (sheep, goat, gazelle, or antelope), the shofar looks as primitive as it is. It is very difficult to play. One's lips must be compressed in just the right way, and adequate wind forced through the horn to make musical tones.

Maimonides asserted that the shofar cried out to sinners to repent, its piercing moan awakening those who slept to examine their misdeeds and turn to righteousness. Others have noted its power to arouse Jews to thoughts of God's power over the world. For it is written that someday "the trumpet will sound," and all Jews shall gather again in the Holy Land to await their deliverance.

So much of Judaism and Jewish practice is centered around the good word or deed. The shofar is one of the most potent of Jewish symbols, a reminder of a time long ago when the shriek of a ram's horn called the faithful to prayer or warriors to combat, fighting for the freedom of Israel and her people.

25

Siddur

Jews were once prohibited from writing down their prayers. Copying blessings down was viewed as akin to burning the Torah. But when the oral tradition was threatened with extinction during the Roman persecutions, the law against written prayer was revoked. Initially, handwritten prayer books were used by the leaders of Jewish communities, primarily for the long and difficult fast day observances. Gradually, this practice extended to include the list of daily prayers and liturgies used for the Sabbath and holidays.

By the ninth century (during the European Dark Ages, a period of widespread illiteracy and superstition), Spanish Jewry had created the first prayer book for services led by a community leader throughout the year. This *Seder Rav Amram Gaon* (written by a Babylonian writer, Amram Gaon) was followed a century later by the Siddur of Saadiah Gaon in Egypt, which was meant for use by individual congregants.

Every year since has brought new prayer books reflecting local traditions and developments in the Jewish community. From the *Mahzor Vitry* during Rashi's time; the *"Great" Mahzor* of the Ashkenazim; and the *Nusah ha-Ari* of the mystic Isaac Luria; to Simeon Singer's *Authorized Daily Prayer Book*; and the *Gates of Prayer—The New Union Prayerbook* and its sister volumes of the American Reform movement, the Siddur has marked the progress of Jewish faith and the communication and continuation of its liturgy.

Jewish literacy ranks among the highest levels in world history, and this is directly related to the preservation of its fundamental prayers in the Siddur. The custom of daily recitation of prayers from a worn prayer book, even perhaps more than the reading from the Torah, has set world Jewry apart from the rest of a less well-read humanity.

26

Talmud

The Talmud took over seven hundred years to compile. A storehouse of law and folklore, it is a compendium of commentary and rabbinical examinations. At its core is the Mishnah, the written version of the Oral Law passed down over the generations since Moses received the word of God at Sinai. Surrounding the Mishnah is the Gemara: discussions, arguments, and debates of rabbis and scholars such as Rashi. Questions are asked, answers proffered, comparable texts cited. The explanations given by Talmudic commentators are sometimes not obviously logical, but often similar to free association. The mix of Biblical stories; practical advice; tales of demons, science, and philosophy; and Greek, Aramaic, Hebrew, and Latin verbiage at times add a human dimension to what could have been an academic exercise. The Talmud has been likened to a living organism, with all its inconsistencies but essential life.

The first Talmud, the so-called Jerusalem Talmud, was completed in the northern part of Israel around 400 C.E. It is only about a third the size of the Babylonian Talmud, which was finished a century later and was acknowledged to be the essential source by sages such as Maimonides. This text, the Babylonian, is the one most commonly referred to today as "the" Talmud.

Despite periodic burnings of the Talmud by Catholic censors from the thirteenth through the sixteenth centuries, the study of Talmud and its preservation by scholars and scribes through the years insured the development of Jewish life. The religious requirement to study Torah (Deut. 6:7 and 11:19) was transformed into the mandate of learning Talmud. Jewry placed its faith in the power of Talmudic analysis and debate, adding a new facet to human thought. During centuries of ignorance and what seemed to be the denial of humanity, the Talmud defined Judaism and the life of its literate adherents.

27

Tefillin

You shall bind them as a sign on your hand and as frontlets between your eyes. . . ." (Deut. 6:8)

The Bible does not indicate, however, how this is to be done. The Oral Law, developed by the sages over the centuries, responded by devising small containers holding sacred parchment that are known in Hebrew as *tefillin*. Tefillin, translated as "phylacteries" in English, are two small leather boxes (*batim*), containing parchment and having leather straps, that are worn on the hand (not the one you write with) (*shel yad*) and the forehead (*shel rosh*).

The text on the parchment held in the *batim* sets forth four sections of the Torah as well as the beginning of the Shema. It contains the basic beliefs of Jews in one God whose rule is unquestioned and through whom the world will be redeemed.

In Orthodox Judaism every male over thirteen is required to wear tefillin at weekday morning services. Since the requirement is time related, women are held to be exempt. However, many feminists wear tefillin as a proud emblem of religious equality, pointing to the story of the daughter of Saul, Michal, who put them on in ancient times without protest from her brethren.

The procedure in donning tefillin is also ritually prescribed. Ashkenazic and Sephardic believers differ in some of the details involved in their application. Yet when the tefillin are wound on the inner arm— "close to the heart"—it is clear what is being expressed.

Like the kippah and *tzitzit* (ritual fringes—see topic number 31), tefillin are proud, *visible*, and mindful symbols of Jews' heartfelt obedience to the Almighty.

28

Temple

"May it be the will of God that the Temple is speedily rebuilt in our time." (Tractate "Tamid" in the *Mishnah*)

The Bible relates that King Solomon built the First Temple on Mount Moriah in Jerusalem largely to house the Ark of the Covenant holding the tablets containing the Ten Commandments in a sacred room called the Holy of Holies —off limits to all but the high priest on Yom Kippur. Solomon's father, King David, had been restrained by the Prophet Nathan from constructing the Temple. Nathan proclaimed God's judgment that David was unfit because he had too much blood on his hands from the many wars he fought to unify the ancient land of Israel.

The First Temple was made of cedar brought from what is now Lebanon, carefully hewn stone, and gold, and was largely a place of priestly ritual and animal sacrifice. The Temple was at the center of most ancient Jewish religious life. It had stood for just over four hundred years when it was destroyed in 586 B.C.E. by the conquering Neb-uchadrezzar who forced the Jews into exile, where they wept by the river of Babylon.

Sixty-five to seventy years later the Second Temple was built. A more imposing structure than the original, it was made even more grand by King Herod four centuries later (just before the period of Hillel and Shammai, the early Christians, and the Judean War). Its destruction by Titus in 70 C.E. is remembered each year on Tisha B'Av. At a Jewish wedding, the joy of the occasion is touched by a moment of sadness with the shattering of a glass by the groom—lest we forget the destruction of Jewry's most holy place.

After the reunification of Jerusalem following the Six-Day War in 1967, Israeli authorities decreed that the Islamic mosques on the Temple Mount where the Second Temple stood would be administered by Muslim authorities. A large plaza was opened up in front of the Western Wall (before 1976, called the Wailing Wall) so the faithful (divided by sex) could congregate in prayer. Orthodox Jews still pray for the rebuilding of the Temple. There is also a small organization in Israel that publicizes and raises money for the construction of a Third Temple. However, the leveling of the Muslim buildings on the site, where it is believed Muhammad the Prophet ascended to Heaven, would lead to an international jihad, or holy war, against Israel. Official Israeli government policy has long opposed this.

In addition to all this controversy, contemporary Orthodox rabbinic opinion holds that Jews must not enter the Temple area because they might walk where the Holy of Holies once stood. For on the most sacred day of the year in ancient times, the most powerful religious figure, the High Priest, would enter the Holy of Holies where the sacred tablets given to Moses on Sinai lay in the Ark and utter (while thinking and feeling only the most pure thoughts so that the world would be saved) the name of He who has no name.

The miracle of Judaism is that it survived the destruction of the Second Temple. Through the portability of Torah and Talmud, the Jewish religion became a faith that could be observed anywhere, anytime. The ritual killing of animals was replaced by the perpetual attention in the Oral Law to the "sacrifice" by Jews of their most base instincts in favor of ethical and moral behavior.

29

The Ten Commandments

The Ten Commandments, given to Moses and the Jewish people at Mount Sinai after their Exodus from Egypt, are not only the foundation of Judaism but of all Western civilization.

There is nothing else quite like them in ancient history. Although the Ten Commandments follow the style of a treaty between nations, the Decalogue (*Aseret Ha-Dibrot* in Hebrew), is a pact between humanity and God. Indeed, the first four commandments are about man's relationship with God, the last six about man's relationship with other men.

There have been many misunderstandings about the meanings of the Ten Commandments.

First, they are not all commandments. The first one simply states that there is only one God, who brought the Israelites out of Egypt, and that they will have no other gods than He. It is not a commandment but a simple statement. Some religious philosophers have implied a commandment in the statement. Others, probably more correctly, view the First Commandment's statement as self-evident and therefore, mandatorily followed. No direction or commandment is needed for something so obvious—that there is only one God and no others.

The restriction in the Second Commandment on creating sculptured (typically called "graven") images of God probably resulted in there having been few Jewish artists until Camille Pissarro, Marc Chagall, and Mark Rothko in recent times. Yet the Second Commandment is clear in its intent. Worshiping calves made of gold or black hawks with human bodies is pagan and leads to lawlessness and depravity (as it certainly did for many ancient cultures).

The Third Commandment—not "taking the Lord's name in vain" as it is most commonly translated—is almost always misinterpreted. It does not mean that one should not say "goddamn it!" It is an admonition to the righteous that they are breaking God's most precious laws when they commit acts of evil in His name. This essential lesson of civilized behavior has been lost on religious fanatics of all faiths for eons. Religious people are here to bring truth to the world, not lies.

The Fourth Commandment, keeping the Sabbath holy and refraining from work on that day (as well as not laboring one's beasts of burden), remains a revolutionary concept. Even today, in developing countries, not only adults, but children, are made to work in sweatshops every day in the most abject conditions. Segregating one day a week from the "reality" of life to be devoted to more spiritual concerns, using the Sabbath's teachings as a beacon for all behavior, is still unattainable for most workers in our totalitarian and technological world.

The remaining commandments direct our activity among ourselves and form the basis of Western law. Honoring one's parents, not murdering (justifiable killing is acceptable, such as self-defense), refraining from adultery (destroying not only the marital bond and the trust and intimacy between man and wife, but the family unit and children's welfare), stealing (what is mine is not yours), speaking falsely about someone else (words can destroy sometimes more than weapons), or coveting a neighbor's possessions (this goes for countries also!), are the cornerstones of our civilization and humanity.

Judaism, unlike Christianity, places its greatest emphasis on the holiness of how we act, not on our ability to just have faith. The Ten Commandments state in a public way what we all should hear.

30

Torah (as Holy Text)

Many have called the Torah the "classic of all classics."

The Torah is not just the written scroll found in the synagogue consisting of the Pentateuch (the Five Books of Moses). Some scholars view the Torah as consisting of both written and oral portions. For them, the written Torah is composed of the Five Books of Moses (called the *Chumash* in Hebrew), tales of the Prophets (*Nevi'im*), and Writings (*Ketuvim*). Added to this Torah is a great and ever-expanding literature. The Mishnah, all of the Aggadah and halakhah (see topics number 62 and number 71), from ancient times to the utterances and responses of today's sages, constitute the complete Torah.

The Oral Law is also Torah. Before it was written down, the Torah was an oral tradition recounted in plain speech to generations. The Oral Law reflects the behavior of a people—their age-old discussions on eternal truths (called "gleanings")—and fills in the gaps, and fleshes out the spirit of the Written Law. The Talmud is some of that Oral Law written down. The Oral Law continues to this day.

Torah means "teaching." In ancient times, after the Torah was read, an explanation of the holy text followed in the lingua franca of the day (Greek or Aramaic). From this tradition came the sermon (a central practice today in both Jewish synagogues and Christian churches).

There are many different ways to approach the study of Torah. Some have taken its message literally (in Hebrew the word for this approach is *peshat*). The early Sadducees and the medieval Karaites held that Scripture must be taken at its word. This unyielding approach has not been influential. In fact, the authority of the lessons of Torah rests in its flexibility. Scholars like Philo of Alexandria and Maimonides welded Hellenic philosophy to Torah and created a powerful synthesis (referred to as *remez*). In contrast, the Kabbalists viewed Torah as a starting place for their mystical visions (*sod*). For the mystics, Torah was a maze of symbols waiting to be uncovered through numerology and ecstasy. The most influential and lasting method of Torah study has been rabbinic midrash (see topic number 13).

Scholars have noted the Torah's similarity to other ancient texts. It is true that the Torah contains phrases used in old Egyptian and Babylonian literature. However, those older texts are devoid of the kind of ethical and religious precepts that lie beneath every word in the Torah. No other ancient scroll from the region has the Torah's concept of monotheism or is as attentive to the needs and hopes of all people.

31

Tzitzit

"Speak unto the children of Israel, and bid them make fringes on the corners of their garments throughout their generations." (Num. 15:38)

Jews are required by the Torah to wear ritual fringes connected to any four-cornered article of clothing they wear. Indeed, these fringes (in Hebrew, *tzitzit*) are attached to the prayer shawl, commonly referred to as the large *tallit* or *tallit gadol*, which is worn, in accordance with custom, mostly by men during almost all morning services. It is established also to wear the large tallit when reading the Torah. In addition, many of the observant wear a small tallit, or *tallit katan*, under their shirt, a custom that has been around for only a few centuries (four-sided garments not being so common in modern times).

The Torah also requires that the tzitzit be seen. This has been taken by most to mean that they are to be worn only when it is light. Therefore, the wearing of the tallit is time sensitive. However, the requirement that the tzitzit be seen is interpreted by many Hasidim and ultra-Orthodox today as something to be literally followed. Tzitzit are worn on top of their shirts and displayed to all who see them as a sign of their obedience to God's edict, and, yes, as a symbol of pride.

Many women today want to wear prayer shawls, as well. This is not only an expression of contemporary feminism—a woman wearing a tallit is also expressing pride in *her* Jewishness and in the equality of her sex before God. She wears the tallit wanting all to see that she is. God commanded us to wrap ourselves in tzitzit. The Lord did not define "us."

PART II

HISTORY

32

Academies

The models for the modern yeshiva (which means "sitting" in Hebrew), or Jewish school, were the ancient Palestinian and Babylonian academies. These academies, centered in the northern part of Israel and in what is now Iraq, were the first organized schools of higher Jewish learning. From about the first century until the thirteenth, the written Torah, Mishnah, Talmud, Responsa (important rabbinical answers to questions posed by the faithful), and the compilation of the Oral Law were defined in towns called Yavneh, Usha, Sepphoris, Bene Berak, Tiberias, Lydda, and Caesarea in Israel and Nehardea, Sura, Pumbedita, and Baghdad in Babylonia.

These academies, particularly the first established by Yochanaan ben Zakkai (who successfully entreated Vespasian, Roman conqueror of the kingdom of Judea, "Give me Yavneh and its sages!"), were patterned after the Sanhedrin. The Sanhedrin had served the Jewish people on the Temple Mount as not only its highest court but also as a place of rabbinic learning and authority.

Before the devastation of Jerusalem, its Temple was the center of religious life. After the brutal destruction of Judea by the Romans, first in 70 C.E. and then almost irrevocably in 135 C.E., and the dispersion of those Jews surviving the massacre and pillage into the Roman Empire, Judaism was threatened with extinction. Out of the rubble of a glorious era, in dusty villages far from the ruins of Jerusalem, came a faith that would endure future catastrophes and desolation.

In small groups of scholars (many of whom toiled as farmers during the day only to rush to the academy for study at night) led by a master, or *gaon* ("excellency" in Hebrew), arcane and profound, trivial and all-encompassing aspects of Jewish law and history were discussed, argued over, cataloged, and *written down*. The intent of these groups of students led by generations of brilliant rabbis was to redefine a religion out of memory. Their success, evidenced particularly by the written Torah, Mishnah, and Talmud, has inspired the beliefs of all of Jewry since. Before the great universities of Oxford and Cambridge, the Sorbonne, Harvard, and Yale, the Palestinian and Babylonian academies were the finest examples of literacy and spiritual leadership in the world.

33

Aliyah

Jews do not emigrate to the land of Israel. Despite Ben-Gurion's clarion call in the 1950s for all Jews in the Diaspora to return to Israel, neither do they return to or "go live" in the Holy Land. They "go up" (*aliyah* in Hebrew).

If they should exit from Eretz Yisrael, they also do not just leave, they "descend." Departing is viewed by tradition as more than a step down.

From the Babylonian captivity five hundred years before the beginning of the Common Era, and especially since the Roman dispersion which began with the destruction of Jerusalem by Titus in 70 C.E., Jewish history can be viewed as one great aliyah. Whether or not Jews live in Israel, it is their home, no other place is, and all Jews to their core (whether they like it or not) know it.

There is pride in knowing where you came from and that you can always go back to your place of origin. However, Jewish history for many centuries was a story of denial. Who could tell any Frenchman or German that he could not go back to his fatherland? During almost two thousand years of persecution, Jews did not have this choice. They were not allowed by their host countries in the Diaspora to flee oppression (including many in the Soviet Union until recently). It was as if the oppressors could not part with their dearly oppressed.

The authors of the Talmud recognized the special nature of aliyah. For them, it was simply better, morally and spiritually, to live in Israel. A spouse could even force a divorce over either's wish to make aliyah, if the other did not join in the journey.

The colonization of modern Israel did not arise solely from an abstract desire for aliyah. Rather, the organized persecution of Jews by European fascists and the denial of human rights for centuries by despotic Arab regimes led to waves of migration. Leaving Nazi Germany, Communist Russia, or medieval Yemen for Israel was definitely a step up.

The pioneering generations before the Second World War, however, did choose of their own volition to settle in the Middle East. Likened by many to the cowboys of the American West, these early settlers brought flowers to the desert, lilies to the valley.

The compelling force of aliyah continues to draw Jews from all over to their proudest place on earth.

34

Ashkenazim/Sephardim

Most modern Jews (except for the Yemenites, who have their own group) trace their backgrounds to northwestern Europe or to the countries that border on the Mediterranean. The roots of Ashkenazic Jews are found in Germany. Sephardic Jews look to Spain for their roots, before their expulsion in 1492 after the terror of the Inquisition.

Sephardic religious practice and lifestyle are much more relaxed than those of the Ashkenazic Jews. Very strict obedience to the Law is a hallmark of Ashkenazic Judaism. That's probably because the societies in which Sephardic Jews flourished for so long were generally more open than the repressive and insulated villages of the Ashkenazim.

Askenazim consider themselves to be the desendants of the Jews of ancient Israel, while Sephardim are identified with the Jews of Babylonia. About 75 percent of world Jewry today is Ashkenazic (90 percent before the Shoah). In Israel today, however, due to a higher birthrate, there are more Sephardic Jews than Ashkenazim. Still, the barriers of disparate religious custom separating the two groups are likely to fade as they assimilate each other's customs. The Sephardic pronunciation of Hebrew is now accepted in most Ashkenazic synagogues.

Sephardic Jews, particularly during the so-called Golden Age of Spain before 1492, excelled in many areas of human interests. Great figures such as Maimonides, Judah Halevi, Solomon ibn Gabirol, Abraham ibn Ezra, and Isaac Abravanel changed the worlds of philosophy, medicine, poetry, commerce, and government. Sephardim as varied as the philosopher Spinoza, the librettist Lorenzo da Ponte (Mozart's best playwright), the scientific boxer Daniel Mendoza, and the politician and novelist Benjamin Disraeli contributed a unique texture to humanity. Sephardic fascination with the mysticism of kabbalistic writings has influenced Ashkenazic groups such as the Hasidim in their religious practices and spiritual ideals.

During the Middle Ages, when illiteracy was widespread throughout Europe, Ashkenazic Jews read, studied the Talmud, and argued its often obscure minutiae in meticulous detail. The Ashkenazim developed a culture that was uniquely civilized. The sweet memories of the shtetl (the Yiddish name for the little villages that dotted the Pale of the Settlement in Poland and Russia) rush forth to us surrounded with feelings of nostalgia and melancholy.

Yet Ashkenazic life was so much greater. Integrated community life, respect for ethical and legal values, the use of Yiddish as a unifying tongue throughout Europe, and the establishment of enduring social institutions permitted Ashkenazic civilization to survive in often openly hostile Christian nations.

The Marranos, or hidden Jews, descended from those who had been forced to convert to Catholicism in Spain, but continued in secret to practice their Judaism; they were the Sephardic equivalent of the Ashkenazim who banded together in forgotten villages.

After the destruction of ancient Judea by the Romans, and in the face of adversity, Sephardim and Ashkenazim created a new Judaism in the foreign lands of the Diaspora.

35

Chosen People

"I will make of you a great nation . . . and all the families of the earth shall bless themselves by you." (Gen. 12:2–3)

Chosen for what?

The concept of chosenness is not separateness. It does not mean racial superiority. It is not a claim for uniqueness. It is believed that God elected to choose the people of Israel to establish a covenant between them for the good of all humanity. Jews are reminded in the Bible to be a "light unto the nations," shining the path for all to follow. Jews certainly did not choose to endure centuries of suffering. Then how and why were they chosen?

The Jews' special relationship with God resulted in their greatest contribution to the world—the belief in monotheism, of *one* God, holy and right. Although both Christianity and Islam also claim their own specialness, there is, of course, no one true faith. Despite what any religious zealot may claim, there can be no monopoly on virtue.

In the Bible, God often chastises His people for their transgressions. They bicker among themselves, battle constantly with others, fail to exhibit the virtue their God-inspired status should bestow. However, it is their very humanness that sets them as examples for all the world. Some rabbis have seen this failed humanity as a sign of decline and degradation.

During periods of crisis and persecution, Jews' recognition of their singular rank has sometimes given them a sense of mission. Seeking excellence, whether spiritually or ethically, is what transfigured a nomadic people into a nation.

Jewish pride can be found in being chosen to remember why we are all here.

36

Christianity

Until the fourth century of the Common Era, they were known as Jewish Christians. That is, for four hundred years after the death of Jesus of Nazareth, his followers still retained a connection in title to their background in Judaism. At early councils, however, the church hierarchy, for political reasons, dropped the Jewish adjective, officially segregating their religion from its past.

Why should Jews today find any pride in their tie with Christianity? The faith of the Jewish Pharisee Saul of Tarsus (known to Christians as St. Paul) has led to brutal anti-Semitism and untold suffering over centuries. Asked to discuss their link with Christianity, Jews may likely point to only negative events: Christian indifference and hostility to their Jewish brethren after the destruction of ancient Judea by the Romans, the massacre of defenseless Jewish villages by knights on their way to the Crusades, the Spanish Inquisition, Martin Luther's call for the burning of European Jewry, the Chmielnicki revolt in the late 1600s in what is now Poland, Czarist pogroms in Russia, and the unique catastrophe of the Shoah. In their exclusive faith in the "one true God," many Christians (and especially their political leaders) seem to have forgotten that others, particularly their Jewish forebears, are also monotheistic believers with comparable ethical concerns.

When a Jewish person enters a church, he immediately notices the absence on the pulpit of the centerpiece of all synagogues—the ark containing Torah scrolls. Instead of the ark there is usually a large cross or, in Mediterranean churches, a massive crucifix with the image of Christ in the agony of death. For Christians, faith in Jesus replaces commitment to Torah. Belief in his resurrection and life everlasting are deemed enough. For Jews, death is only a part of life. Life, and how we spend it, is what is worth celebrating.

Yet not all of Judaism's messages to the world were forgotten by Christians, and this is where pride and commonality can be found. The teachings of Jesus are remarkably similar to those of the great Jewish sage, Rabbi Hillel. Indeed, Jesus may have heard or even been a student of Hillel, for they lived at the same time and the Jewish community in Judea at the time was not all that large. Certainly the ideas of Hillel and his great rival Shammai filtered throughout Judean society during their lifetimes.

The Golden Rule that Jesus taught, whether stated in the negative or positive ("do unto" or "do not do unto"), still promotes brotherhood. It is a message too many over the centuries could not or refused to hear. If there is to be an end to anti-Semitism and Jewish prejudice against Christians, it will only come when Jew and Christian recognize that their faiths grew from the same roots.

37

Diaspora

Diaspora is the Greek word for dispersion. It has been associated with the concepts of exile and captivity. Yet there is a difference between being exiled and being dispersed.

Jewish historians point to the four-hundred-year captivity in Babylonia as the first diaspora. "By the river of Babylon, there we sat down. Yea, we wept when we remembered Zion," sings the psalmist. Abraham had predicted this incarceration of a whole people. Kept in Babylon for a dozen generations, the First Temple lying in ruins, the Ark of the Covenant lost, still, somehow, the Jewish people stayed together, and when they were ready to return to ancient Israel, they were still Jews.

The Judean Wars of 70 and 135 C.E. resulted in the next, more lasting dispersion, what is commonly known as the Diaspora with a capital *D*. The Jewish nation was scattered, mostly in slavery, to the far reaches of the Roman Empire. Herod's Temple, known as the Second Temple, lay in ruins. Jews adapted over the next almost two thousand years to their new cultures, and these new cultures often changed for the better because they were there.

The prominence of Arabic kingdoms throughout the Middle Ages was strengthened by the presence of great thinkers and healers such as Maimonides; the glory of Spain reflected the poetry of Judah Halevi; the rise of industrialism and modern commerce was made richly vibrant by the Rothschilds; German music and literature were sanctified by Mendelssohn and Mahler, Heine and Kafka; and physical and psychological realities were made plain by Einstein and Freud.

In their dispersion away from a central temple, away from what they had thought was their gateway to God, Jews essentially created a new religion. With the destruction of the Second Temple and the Diaspora, Judaism became a portable religion. Memorize the Torah, write it down when you get to wherever you have to go, and then build a structure to house its sacred words.

The development of the Written Law and of Talmudic writings brought the spirit of God into exile. The "Divine Presence in exile" (*Shekhinta be-Galuta*) inspired different kinds of people to observe a common religious heritage.

Exile can mean that there is no way back. Diaspora connotes that for Jewish believers the way back is before them in observance and remembrance.

38

Disputations

After the destruction of Judea by the Romans in 135 C.E. and before the restoration of the State of Israel in 1948, almost two thousand years later, Jews often lived in societies openly hostile to their very presence. During what have become known as the "disputations," prominent rabbis (the most famous of them Rabbi Moses ben Nahman, popularly known to the observant by the acronym Ramban, or Nahmanides of Gerona, Spain) were put on public display in defense of their religion often against apostate Jews. These debates before large groups of the Christian majority (small groups of Jews were sometimes allowed to attend) were designed by their oppressors to sway Jewish people to convert, or to at least challenge their beliefs.

During these challenges, the essential practices and value system of Judaism were put into question by those who would deny its right to exist. Indeed, the Disputation at Barcelona in 1263, in which Nahmanides participated with the converted Jew (probably from southern

France) Pablo Christiani, took place during a period of growing persecution that led to the rise of the grand Inquisitors and the fall of Spanish culture and influence. Other famous debates between Jews and Christians over the centuries include those between Moses Mendelssohn and Johann Lavater in the eighteenth century and between Martin Buber and Karl Ludwig Schmidt during the twentieth.

These debates on the relative merits of Christianity and Judaism were originated by Catholic priests desiring to disgrace the most prominent Jewish leaders and their beliefs. Strict limitations were imposed on what the Jewish debaters could say. How the disputations would conclude was therefore preordained. Brutality was threatened for those not following the prepared script. Indeed, the disputation in Paris in 1240 led directly to the burning of handwritten Talmudic manuscripts.

The questions asked at these disputations usually involved Torah and Talmud. Yet the answers sought could not be found in these sacred texts. Rather, the Christian interrogators tried to prove how Judaism had predicted their Messiah.

To their everlasting credit (and despite great personal danger), the Jews who participated in the disputations usually prevailed in their arguments. Using logic, scripture, and common sense drawn from real life, the rabbis upheld the integrity of their religion. Their pride in their Judaism carried them through the fire of bigotry.

39

Exodus

"I am the Lord, your God, who brought you from the land of Egypt."
(Lev. 11:45)

Jews are required to remember their Exodus from Egypt every day
(see Deut. 16:3). As part of the daily Shema, Jews remember that their
God brought them out of Egypt to be their God.

The Jewish exodus from the oppression of Raamses, the greatest
and most powerful of the Egyptian pharaohs, was the first and only
successful rebellion in the ancient world. When Jews were cast adrift in
the almost-two-thousand-year Diaspora after the Judean Wars in 70
and 135 C.E., they remembered every day, and especially every Passover,
that there was a way to freedom. Liberty resided in faith.

The lesson of this flight into freedom has inspired all of humanity.
Jews can proudly claim that theirs is a religion where all are equal before
God and that no one has the right to subjugate another. These affirma-
tions are, of course, the basis of what we think of as civilization. Jewish
values conceived in the heat of flight are still instructing the world.

40

Golden Age of Spanish Jewry

Jews had lived in Spain for many centuries before the invasion of the Iberian peninsula by Islamic forces in 711 C.E. First brought to Spain by Roman forces, Jews had lived under a despotic Visigoth rule for hundreds of years. When the Muslim forces invaded, they came as conquering heroes. Jews fought with the Muslims against their Christian oppressors, assisting in the Islamic takeover of most of the country. An exceptional tenth century Jewish leader, Hasdai ibn Shaprut, worked with the Muslim leaders in negotiating peace treaties and established Jewry's importance to the country's new rulers.

Under a series of remarkably lenient caliphs for the next three hundred years, Jews attained positions of major significance. In many ways this period was as fruitful for Jewish history as contemporary American Jewish times have been. Jews were allowed in large measure to practice their faith and to express their innermost thoughts in artistic works. Some Jews amassed great fortunes and served the state in high political offices.

Many historians, however, have remarked that the Golden Age was not always so golden. For example, when a radical Islamic group, the Almohades, invaded Spain and Morocco in the twelfth century, many Jews were killed or forced to flee. The most famous—and most important—of these refugees was Moses ben Maimon, or Maimonides, the greatest Jewish philosopher. One hundred years before, in 1066, a Muslim mob murdered four thousand Jews in a bloodbath in Granada.

Yet, relative to the continual death, degradation, and darkness that engulfed Jews in most of the rest of Europe during the Middle Ages, Islamic Spain provided a safe haven for a life of peace and prosperity. A prosperous existence often leads to contemplation and aesthetics.

This milieu of religious toleration and economic opportunity enabled poetry of extraordinary expressivity to flower. Solomon ibn Gabirol, Moses ibn Ezra, and Judah Halevi are among a group of remarkable poets and commentators from this era. In the works of Halevi there can even be found strains of Zionism. Many of their works, in fact, influenced Christian philosophers and theologians.

The Golden Age shines so brightly because the rest of Europe was so dark with hopelessness. The accomplishments of Spanish Jews are glorious examples of the power of Jewish expression when left alone to bloom.

41

Hasidism

The example of one individual—his unique influence—can sometimes change history.

So it was with the remarkable life of the Master of the Good Name, Rabbi Israel ben Eliezer, also known as Baal Shem Tov and affectionately called the Besht.

Until his arrival in the 1700s, Ashkenazic Jews throughout Europe shared a common tradition. They prayed the same way, had similar customs, and emphasized the central role of the Torah for all Jewish experience. Despite the tight and richly developed society that was Ashkenazic Jewry's lot, there was still widespread anti-Semitism among their host Gentile nations. Faced with the unrelenting Gentile hatred of Jews and unable to expect any improvement to their mostly mundane lives in the Pale of the Settlement (the area in which Jews were restricted to live in Russia by czarist authorities), many Jews had lost their will to live.

The Besht changed all that.

"A river flowed out of Eden to water the garden: It then split and became four branches." (Gen. 2:10). From the exuberant example of the Besht flowed his great disciples, men with names like Elimelech of Lyzhansk, Israel of Kozienice, Meir of Apta, Menahem Mendel of Rymanow, and the Seer of Lublin, Jacob Isaac. Out of these men came the great Nahman of Bratislava and Menahem Mendel of Kotsk. Dynasties of Hasidim were often named for the towns in which their great leaders lived and taught—Belz ("mein shtetele Belz," as the old song goes), Bobova, Gur, Satmar, Vizhnitz, and the most famous, Lubavich (Chabad).

They had in common their connection with the Besht and his joyous outlook on life. Despite the decade (or century), they remained clothed in the garb of Polish noblemen of the Besht's time (an ironic way to dress considering that these Poles subjugated and largely detested their people). All spoke Yiddish, and all congregated before their leader, often called "rebbe," to gather morsels of knowledge, to be nourished by the rich diet of his thought. To them, the rebbe was the only gateway to righteousness.

The Hasidim introduced a special magic to Jewish observance, a belief in holy men (Tzaddikim) who journeyed about the world righting wrongs and bringing light unto the darkness. Until the scholarly influence of their opposition, the so-called *Mitnagdim*, infiltrated Hasidism, they sought God more in rapturous prayer than in Torah study. Hasidim saw God everywhere. Some called it pantheism—the unity of one Supreme Being threatened by the wild intensity of Hasidism.

The threat to both Hasidim and Mitnagdim created by the Jewish Enlightenment, or *Haskalah* (see topic number 42), led Hasidism away from its local roots (and, some would say, unique vitality) to a concern with upholding tradition. Without the pipe-smoking model of the Baal Shem Tov, the people obviously needed more direction.

All Jews should find comfort in Hasidism's quest for spiritual joy. There is no greater happiness than fulfilling with vigor the commandments of God.

42

Haskalah

There are some who view the Haskalah, or Jewish Enlightenment—the desire to connect with the secular world—as the beginning of the end of traditional Judaism. Were it not for strict Orthodoxy and its refusal to associate with Gentile society (except for limited trade), the Jewish religion would surely perish, they argue.

The Haskalah arose out of the emancipation during Napoleonic times of most of Europe's Jews. This shock into freedom led to assimilation for much of Jewry in the countries of Western Europe. Before the Shoah, German Jews often asserted that they were Germans first, Jews second. French Jews still assert their primary attachment to their proud country. Yet the attachment to the secular and non-Jewish culture of European countries has not been only a negative concern. For many, especially those who participate in Reform synagogues, the combination of everyday life with spiritual observance has enriched their Jewish identities—and pride.

It was the Jewish Enlightenment that reestablished the use of ancient Hebrew as the language of Israel. Yiddish, despite its rich vocabulary, has been viewed until recently as a language of the oppressed. However, the proud use of Hebrew as the Jewish lingua franca helped result in the Zionist ideal and the founding of the State of Israel.

The Haskalah movement has also integrated secular life with Jewish living. It recognizes that Jews must adapt to the changes of the modern world. By being part of a wider society one could find liberation from the strictures of Orthodoxy. Studying not just Jewish history but the history of all peoples and immersing oneself in secular subjects, not just religious ones, has expanded the consciousness and aspirations of Jewish observers. To participate in a public airing of the successes and failures of the Enlightenment has improved the minds of Jews while raising for them the questions all contemporary people face. For example, how to retain an ethnic and religious background (often they are one and the same) in an America where melting into the "pot" is favored, but being different is also protected.

The Haskalah influenced Jews lost in the prejudice of Europe to return to Zion. Theodor Herzl, the founder of modern Zionism, was, for example, a largely assimilated Austrian Jew. Nevertheless, his association with Gentiles in Vienna, his revulsion at the anti-Semitic prosecution of Alfred Dreyfus in France, and the liberating nature of his mind, led him to the Zionist ideal. A shtetl Jew in Russia, unexposed to the complexities and power of the industrialized world, would never have thought up Zionism.

43

"Hatikvah"

"Next year in Jerusalem!"

This saying, repeated by Jews in the Diaspora for almost two thousand years, found its artistic expression in the poem, and later national anthem of Israel, "Hatikvah" (in English, "The Hope"). The music and words of "Hatikvah" have a special resonance for every Jew.

Naftali Hertz Imber, a Hebrew poet, wrote the words to "Hatikvah." In the 1880s his poem was set to music by one Samuel Cohen, newly arrived in Palestine. The music for "Hatikvah" was inspired by a Moldavian-Romanian folk song that also formed the basis for Bedrich Smetana's tone poem, "Vltava" (commonly known in English as "The Moldau"). For years, even learned musicologists thought the song had indigenous roots in Jewish culture and was not the arrangement it in fact is. "Hatikvah" was sung at several Zionist congresses led by Theodor Herzl and then David Wolfssohn, and gradually came to be accepted as the official song of a Jewish people actively yearning for the restoration of their nationhood.

The folk melody of "Hatikvah" begins in a minor key (usually played in D minor) and rises up to a related major key (usually F major) before it falls back into a minor at its end. The music reflects the hope for a return to Zion that so haunted world Jewry before the restoration of the State of Israel. With Israel's rise to its high place among the world's nations, "Hatikvah" now represents for Jews a hope for peace, expressed in wishful words and moving melody, that all people can live free in their own land.

Kol od ba·lel·vav pe·ni·ma,
ne·fesh Ye·hu·di ho·mi·ya.
U·le·fa·a·tei miz·rach ka·di·ma,
a·yin le·tsi·yon tso·fi·ya.

Od lo a·ve·da tik·va·tei·nu,
ha·tik·va she·not al·pa·yim,
li·he·yot am chof·shi be·ar·tsei·nu,
be·e·rets tsi·yon vi·ru·sha·la·yim.

כָּל עוֹד בַּלֵּבָב פְּנִימָה
נֶפֶשׁ יְהוּדִי הוֹמִיָּה,
וּלְפַאֲתֵי מִזְרָח קָדִימָה
עַיִן לְצִיּוֹן צוֹפִיָּה.

עוֹד לֹא אָבְדָה תִקְוָתֵנוּ,
הַתִּקְוָה שְׁנוֹת אַלְפַּיִם,
לִהְיוֹת עַם חָפְשִׁי בְּאַרְצֵנוּ,
בְּאֶרֶץ צִיּוֹן וִירוּשָׁלַיִם.

44

Islam

"There is no god but Allah, and Muhammad is His prophet."

Islam shares with Judaism a faith in one, indivisible God. Unlike the Christian concept of a Holy Trinity, and unlike its graphic representation of God with crucifixes, statues, and stained glass, Islam is an abstract religion like Judaism. Graven images are banned, periodic worship and charitable acts mandated.

Like Judaism, Islam is a highly regulated faith. Every act a person takes is subject to God's laws. Whether it be how one acts in society, eats, conducts prayer, metes out justice, or raises a family; it is all spelled out in legal and moral regulation and spoken tradition. Based upon an oral law like Judaism, Islamic tradition was transformed over centuries into scripture. The core of Islam is morally and profoundly ethical. Indeed, much of the faith was developed in Babylonia (now Iraq) at the same time the Jewish Talmud was compiled. Neither religion has a monopoly on moral teachings.

The Koran, like the Bible, relates how the forefathers of the religion came to their beliefs. The Prophet Muhammed, whose very name is blessed to all Muslims, called himself the Messenger of God and the Seal of the Prophets. He viewed himself not as the initiator of a new faith but as one who was sent here by God to ratify the Bible. The word *Koran* itself is a kind of confirmation of the Hebrew language. Derived from the Hebrew and Aramaic word *mikra* used by Jews to signify Torah, the Koran contains many references to the Jewish prophets, especially to Abraham. Abraham is viewed not only as the father of Ishmael, from whom all Arabs are descended, but also as the first believer in one God, called Allah.

The Jewish-Muslim relationship over the centuries has been complicated. Long periods of Islamic subjugation of Jewish freedoms were tempered by periods of great economic growth and artistic achievement (the so-called Golden Age of Spain). More recently, the conflicts in the Middle East have rendered a pall over the relations of the two faiths. With Jews and Christians attempting to find much needed common ground fifty years after the Shoah, there is still much to be done to break down prejudices and fears between Jews and Muslims, who share so much of which they can both be proud.

45

Israel Defense Forces

The comedian Jackie Mason has joked that no one is scared of a single Jew, but put them together in an army, and they'll kill you.

The Israel Defense Forces (*Tzahal* in Hebrew) is considered by many to be the best fighting force for its size in the world. Surely it has needed to be. In six major wars over almost thirty-five years—the 1948 War of Independence, the Suez War of 1956, the Six-Day War in 1967, the War of Attrition against Egypt (1968–70), the 1973 Yom Kippur War, and the Lebanese invasion in 1982—the IDF has faced Arab armies whose numbers far exceeded it. Despite the odds, the IDF succeeded each time in defending Israel against its enemies.

The IDF was created by Israel's first prime minister, David Ben-Gurion, from four distinct groups that had fought for the creation of the State of Israel and sometimes had battled with each other. These four groups, the Palmach, Haganah, Irgun, and Lekhi, had different origins, but the same goal—the establishment of an independent Jewish state. It has been the IDF's special role to preserve that state.

Its unique strength lies in the service of most Israeli men and women in its forces.

Although the active units are small in number (only about 140,000 people), the IDF counts on its reserves for its full power. Reservists can be called up on forty-eight-hour notice. Anwar Sadat's surprise attack on Israel during Yom Kippur in 1973 showed the weakness and then the incredible might of the IDF. Due to a thirty-year period of reserve duty and annual training, the Israeli fighting force is constantly being tuned to be in top fighting shape. Every action it takes in defense of the nation is felt immediately back home, for home is usually only minutes away. This closeness to friends and family has contributed to making the IDF's role unique in modern warfare. The immediacy of battle to the home causes everything the IDF does to be real, never abstract. Defense of Israel does not occur in places like Flanders Fields or Okinawa. The proximity of soldiers' families to their place of work makes what this largely reserve army does deeply personal and firsthand.

Being a soldier carries tremendous responsibility. Being an Israeli soldier in the IDF has an importance to the Jewish people that is incalculable.

46

Jerusalem

"If I forget thee, O Jerusalem. . . ."

Jews have never forgotten Jerusalem. The capital of Israel is more than the geographic heart of the Jewish people. Jerusalem was chosen by David as the center of his kingdom. Solomon built the First Temple there to house the Ark of the Covenant in its holiest of holies. The Persians laid siege to its walls. The Maccabbees fought Hellenic Syrians for its control. Zealots battled Romans, leading to its destruction. Crusaders massacred Muslims and Jews in its squares. Israelis unified the city during the Six-Day War in 1967 and restored it to glory. The story of Jerusalem largely parallels the story of the Jewish people and much of Western history. Within its gates were born three great religions, and outside its boundaries began the Diaspora.

Jerusalem is considered by Jewish tradition to be the holiest place on earth (and on the Temple Mount, the Holy of Holies, the most sacred). Jerusalem has always been a place to come back to, not to leave.

During ancient times, three pilgrimages per year were required of men to make sacrifice to God. "Next year in Jerusalem" was the clarion call of generations spread throughout the dispersion; most were unable to return, yet they remembered.

Indivisible capital of the Jewish state, site of the First and Second Temples, symbol of religious faith, more than a city, Jerusalem is the spiritual center of the world. Not Cairo, Paris, London, Washington, Moscow, New Delhi, or Beijing has its immediate significance. No wonder so many have fought over its ownership.

Jews are proud of their city, their Jerusalem. So much so that the Israeli government has guaranteed access to holy sites to all religious groups with roots in the city. No other government has done as much for so many varied creeds. With so many religions vying for a piece of its rock, it is not surprising that Israeli control of Jerusalem has attracted world attention and often jealous criticism.

Even as Jerusalem is the place of Jesus' last days and the Prophet Muhammad's ascension to heaven, it remains the emotional and spiritual core of the Jewish body. There is still Torah and Talmud without Jerusalem. The Temple is found in every synagogue across the globe. But the City of God, the Paragon of Beauty, the Lion of God where truth be found, endures as the focal point of Jewish life on earth.

47

The Jewish 100

The inspiration to write *Jewish Pride* was largely derived from my experiences speaking to Jewish audiences about my first book, *The Jewish 100: A Ranking of the Most Influential Jews of All Time*. The reaction to *The Jewish 100* was overwhelmingly positive. At last a book, people exclaimed, not on the suffering of the Jews but about their achievements! The Torah, not persecution, has defined who we are and what we have done in this world.

The one hundred people comprising the list, each born of a Jewish mother, changed the way we live and think. This applies to all people, not just Jews. Their accomplishments are in every field of human endeavor, and included among them are central figures in the human experience such as Moses, Abraham, Maimonides, Einstein, Freud, Spinoza, Anne Frank, and Mahler. The test—born of a Jewish mother—led to some controversial choices.

The inclusion in the book of three so-called Jewish Christian figures—Jesus of Nazareth, Mary, and St. Paul (Saul of Tarsus)—was surprising to most, but almost heretical to others. Yet their role in the civilization of everyone's world cannot be ignored. The Judaic, Hillel-inspired message of much of Christianity should give Jews some pride. This, of course, would come more easily were it not for the terrible history that still separates the two religious groups.

Other choices were less troublesome and even amusing. Jewish contributions to the arts are so varied and interesting that the choosing became almost a contest. Yet, to find the person who represents the core of a branch of our experience became the overriding purpose of the book. For example, when researching feminism, it became clear that with her clear sense of purpose Betty Friedan fueled the engine that drove women to seek equality. Casimir Funk's vitamins led to modern concerns with nutrition. The integration of jazz into classical forms by George Gershwin gave fresh direction to American music. The only Jewish prime minister in British history, Benjamin Disraeli, established an empire that brought parliamentary democracy to the far reaches of the globe. All were Jewish, not necessarily religious, yet ultimately spiritual in their intent.

Jewish people should feel immensely proud of the positive attainments of their influential 100.

48

Khazars

During the Middle Ages in the southern region of central Russia lived a fierce people called the Khazars. These Caucasian people were known as mighty fighters (similar to the Afghan warriors of today who defeated the Russian Army).

At the end of the eighth century, the Khazar king Bulan and a collection of nobles sought to inculcate their warlike culture with some spirituality. They invited into their kingdom three representatives of Judaism, Christianity, and Islam, and asked them to publicly debate the merits of their respective religions. The Jewish teacher won their hearts and minds, and Judaism became the official religion of Khazar. By the eleventh century the Khazar kingdom was invaded and destroyed, yet the memory of this remote, powerful, and *independent* Jewish state lingered in the collective thoughts of Jews for centuries.

It was thought until recently that the Khazar kingdom was a fantasy of the Spanish poet Judah Halevi. His fiction, *The Kuzari*, was the basis for much of Jewish remembrance of this compelling chapter in Jewish history.

Modern research has revealed, however, that there was a mass Khazarian conversion to Judaism and widespread Jewish practices among the Khazars.

This example encouraged the rest of Jewry during the Middle Ages that the successes of Christians and Muslims, often at the cost of wide-scale Jewish suffering, were temporary. Jews too could have a kingdom, mystical and remote though the Khazars may have seemed.

49

Knesset

The Israeli legislature, the Knesset, is modern Jewry's proudest example of democracy. Comprised of one hundred twenty members, the Knesset is a single legislative body—a combined House of Representatives and Senate, if you will.

Members of the Knesset are not elected individually. Proportional representation—the election of parties who designate their own membership in the legislature—has resulted in a system favoring a wide disparity of political opinion. Although two major parties, Labor and Likud, are the most prominent, they rely on smaller groups to form coalition governments and assert their power.

These smaller parties in the Knesset represent the ultra-Orthodox, with ambiguous feelings about Zionism; Sephardim concerned about the upholding of their traditions in a secular Israel; right-wing nationalists; Soviet emigres; Communists; and Arabs. The Knesset is a remarkable microcosm of Israeli society. All Israeli citizens over eighteen years of age, regardless of background, are eligible to vote for the parties of their choice. Members sit for four years (or less, if elections are called earlier).

The Knesset is a rather raucous place. Like the House of Commons in Great Britain, the head of state and his or her ministers sit in the Knesset available to immediate criticism from political opponents. The immediacy of having the prime minister in the Knesset often leads to contentious argument.

Yet in the Middle East, where many governments are nondemocratic (and some tyrannical), the example of the Knesset—true democracy in action—sets Israel apart.

50

Marranos

Imagine yourself believing in something that you cannot share with anyone other than your family. Suppose that if you do share that faith with someone you trust, you may be betrayed, dragged before the authorities, interrogated, tortured, forced to foreswear your beliefs or face being impaled or burned at the stake.

Jews in Spain and Portugal from the fourteenth century until (incredibly!)1834 were unable to practice their religion openly. The only way they could live as Jews was in secret. Subject to an inquisition of unyielding hate, fearful for their very lives, those Spanish and Portuguese Jews who did not yield to Christianity literally went underground. They became hidden Jews, swine (*marranos*) in the eyes of their oppressors, but hidden converts (*anusim*) in their own hearts.

A public Jewish life in Spain and Portugal did not survive the Inquisition. Jewish religious practices conducted in secret became diluted. The remembrance of the communal act of Jewish prayer was rendered dim by the overwhelming force of organized bigotry.

Yet despite waves of persecution, from the deaths of fifty thousand Jews by mobs in Castile and Aragon in 1391 to the public auto-da-fé of the Spanish Inquisition after 1480; and although over one hundred thousand Jews chose baptism instead of martyrdom; Jews fled to Portugal, North Africa, Italy, Greece, and Turkey and established a Sephardic diaspora that energized Mediterranean trade and culture. Many of those who remained sought to remain Jews, at least in spirit. Known as "conversos," or Jews converted to Christianity, they still remained subject to dangerous inquisition and being revealed as Judaizers by their persecutors. The weight of centuries of institutional hatred buried Jewish life in Spain and Portugal (despite traces of Judaic practices still evident in remote places in Mexico and Portugal as late as the early twentieth century).

Jewish religious tradition is kind to those who would be made martyrs. The preservation of life is always the first priority. Again, imagine if not only yourself but also your children were faced with slaughter or forced conversion. What would you do?

Jews today must remember with pride those who perished in the flames for their beliefs as well as those who hid from the raging fires, still keeping the eternal light alive in their spirit.

51

Masada

Until a reawakening of poetic and archeological interest during the twentieth century, the story of Masada was buried in the rocks and mountains in the Dead Sea region.

Seventy years after the beginning of what is known as the Common Era, the Zealots, rebels who had risen up against their Roman oppressors during the Great Revolt, made a final stand at the mountaintop fortress built by King Herod at Masada. For three years the 960 defenders held off the overwhelming force of the Roman Tenth Legion. Each day the Romans fortified their position, building battle works designed to overcome the high natural defenses of Masada (the only entrance to the fortress was through a snake path). Finally, faced with imminent defeat, the Zealots chose suicide, killing their children, wives, and then themselves, rather than be sold into slavery and prostitution.

The story of Masada was forgotten for centuries, not mentioned in the Talmud or other sacred texts. The rabbis who wrote the Talmud and sought to create a portable religion not reliant on politics and state-hood may have wanted to distance themselves from fighters. The only contemporaneous account is found in Josephus' *The Jewish Wars*, a Roman-style history written by a Jewish collaborator hated by the Zealots.

To Jews today, Masada is not a story about suicide. Rather, especially for Israelis (and anyone who has walked up that narrow path to the top of the fortress), it's a symbol of survival. For despite overwhelmingly superior Roman forces, a small group of Zealots kept at bay hardened Imperial troops for a lengthy period of time. These Jewish fighters defeated the Romans by their deaths as liberated people.

When Gen. Yigal Yadin and his team of archeologists unearthed Masada in the 1960s, they discovered the skeletons of twenty-five men, women, and children. Two years after the Six-Day War in 1969, these defenders of ancient Judea were buried with full military honors by their successors, on Masada in a free Israeli state.

52

Our Crowd

Stephen Birmingham's brilliant book, *Our Crowd*, brought to the attention of the world (and especially to Jews of Eastern European origins) the importance of the great, mostly German families whose enormous wealth and social position transformed American society and its retail, banking, and communications industries. Guggenheim, Rosenwald, Straus, Warburg, Schiff, Seligman, Goldman, Sachs, Loeb, Lehman, Bloomingdale, Altman, Ochs, and Sulzberger are some of the names of these families.

This "crowd" began to make its fortune during the Civil War. Bankers such as Joseph Seligman and Jacob Henry Schiff contributed to the development and the reliability of America's financial institutions. However, even these Jews were largely restricted from the industries that fueled the explosive growth of America: railroads, chemicals, steel, shipping, oil, and utilities. Sales provided the easiest entry into financial freedom. Retail giants such as Macy's (founded by Isidor Straus) gave Americans what they needed at affordable prices.

Their importance in the founding of Jewish institutions in America also should not be underestimated. Despite an early anti-Zionist bent of some of these families, many of the most prominent Jewish institutions of today, such as the American Jewish Committee, the Union of American Hebrew Congregations, and Hebrew Union College (and the creation of American Reform Judaism), were begun with their active support.

Many of these great German-Jewish families established charitable foundations or organized assistance for the needy. Their philanthropy seemed to have no bounds. They applied unusual enterprise and creativity to giving. Julius Rosenwald, who in essence founded the modern Sears, Roebuck Company and created the mail-order catalog, considered a life devoted to philanthropic aims man's primary goal. It was not enough to give; making others contribute in a sharing of charity added up to more help for those in need. In addition, these families gave mightily to the museums and symphony orchestras that spread culture to a young nation.

Indeed, their giving yielded these donors their largest riches, setting them apart as an example of a crowd other Jews could emulate, sharing their pride in benevolence.

53

Rescue

The Talmud states unequivocally that "each Jew is responsible for every other Jewish person."

For centuries the rabbis have held that the rescue of a fellow Jew from harm is one of the most blessed acts. However, such rescue should not result in placing another Jew in harm's way. Ransom can be paid. Even paying ransom with holy scrolls is permissible (although it is doubtful modern terrorists would have much interest in Torah).

Pidyon shevuyim (the ransoming of captives) is an ancient concept. "You shall not stand idly by when your neighbor's blood is spilt" (Lev. 19:16). Both the philosopher Maimonides and the codifier Joseph Caro concur that standing idle while another is held captive is the same as harming him yourself.

In recent years, the plight of Jewish airline passengers held at Entebbe Airport in Uganda and their rescue by Israeli commandos is the model all other rescue operations can be compared to. Operation

Solomon, the airlift of besieged Ethiopian Jewry, or the support of Soviet refuseniks, are but two other recent examples of pidyon shevuyim.

Strangers to Judaism might think that concern for captives comes from a certain clannish behavior among Jews or a sharing of common suffering. This is not so. The holding of captives is not only a direct threat to all Jewish existence, but to civilization and to God's law. It simply must be countered, ended by paying some price, whether it be financial (the payment of an actual ransom) or political (the freeing of prisoners or the exchange of bodies of fallen enemies). How to respond to the ransoming of captives—an ancient problem still very much with us—remains a dilemma, but also an obligation which must be addressed.

54

Sabras

Even before the Judean War of 70 C.E. and Rome's dispersion of the survivors into her empire, there was a Jewish Diaspora. Perhaps as many as two million Jews lived outside of ancient Israel along the Mediterranean and as far away as India. During this period, the great city of Alexandria in Egypt boasted a population of half a million Jews. Before the Teutons invaded Germany, Cologne was settled by the Romans and by Jewish traders. Yet, all of Diaspora Jewry felt a connection to the Temple in Jerusalem, which remained at the core of their religion and heritage.

There has always been something special about being born in Israel. After the fall of the Second Temple, and with the writing of the Talmud, Judaism became a portable religion. It mattered little where one was, because human behavior and the way one should act remained constant. Dietary laws could be adapted to the local availability of foodstuffs. People preferred loving-kindness all over. But some felt that one gained an extra edge or a sense of pride and responsibility when born in Israel.

In the almost two thousand years of Diaspora since the fall of Jerusalem to the Romans, few Jews were allowed to settle in Israel. Some pilgrims ventured to the Holy Land at the end of their days with the expectation that they would be buried there. For when the end of the world comes, those buried on the Mount of Olives are supposed to be the first to meet the Final Judgment.

Before the establishment of the Jewish state in 1948, Israel was not a safe haven. The first people the Crusaders massacred after they took Jerusalem in the Crusades were its Jews. Thereafter, under Islamic rule small numbers of Jews were permitted to settle in Israel just so long as they did not make too much of a presence. The random killing of over three dozen Jews by Arabs in Hebron during a 1938 riot attests to a precarious existence even during modern times.

The sabra, or native-born Israeli, has made the Jewish state a reality. The first baby born on the one of the first kibbutzim was the future general, war hero, and defense minister, Moshe Dayan. Future leaders Yitzhak Rabin and Benjamin Netanyahu were also born in Israel. Their parents and grandparents came to Israel mostly as pioneers. The early settlers arrived with a purpose—to settle the land and have children. Unlike previous generations who had come to die, these Jews had come to live.

55

Six-Day War

We studied maps of towns and banks, gulfs and straits, heights and valleys. We were more proud to be Jewish than we had ever been in our lives. After six days of preemptive strikes by air and relentless fighting on the mountains and in the streets, the Israel Defense Forces had crushed the combined military strength of the entire Arab world.

All wars are cauldrons of death and brutality. Most soldiers who have seen combat never want to talk about it. They often say that there is nothing to be proud of. Either you killed or were killed, they simply relate.

The Six-Day War, like most wars, was not necessary. Thousands of Egyptians, Jordanians, Syrians, and their supporters from Saudia Arabia, Iraq, Kuwait, Algeria, and Sudan did not have to perish in an almost Old Testament cataclysm. Peace in the Middle East should not be so illusory for peoples of common background.

For whatever purposes of hate and power grabbing, despots use war to preserve and consolidate their positions. When a nation is organizing for war, the problems of its people, their poverty, lack of education and medical services, housing and financial security, can be forgotten in the battle cry for someone else's blood. Gamal Abdel Nasser, Egypt's president and the founder of its modern government, along with King Hussein of Jordan and leaders of the other Arab states, sought to purge the Middle East of its Jews. Despite Israeli successes in the War of Independence in 1948 and in the Suez War of 1956, the Arabs still thought they could "push the Jews into the Sea."

The immediate period before the Six-Day War was frightening for Israelis. They knew that the Shoah could happen again. The world had not cared once. Why should it care twenty years later?

On June 5, 1967, the Israeli government reacted to Nasser's closing of the Gulf of Aqaba (Israel's main shipping route) as an act of aggression. In one day the Israeli air force destroyed all of Egypt's and most of Syria's planes. During the next five days, IDF ground forces invaded the Sinai, the West Bank, including East Jerusalem, and surged up the Golan Heights, Syria's catbird seat overlooking the kibbutzim and towns of northern Israel.

Because of Israel's refusal to use artillery to secure the sacred lanes of the Old City of Jerusalem, her casualties were extremely high. While the Wailing Wall, the western wall of the Second Temple, and other holy sites were restored to the Jewish state, the fighting claimed 679 Israeli lives, a numbing loss to a small population.

Rather than tame resentments, hardliners in the Arab countries continued to escalate the conflict with Israel. The Yom Kippur War in 1973, ongoing terrorism, Lebanese invasions, and the intifada have followed. We all pray for peace and the end of bloodletting.

After thousands of years of persecution and massacre and despite setbacks since, the fact that Israelis could fight back with such Biblical ferocity in the Six-Day War energized contemporary Jewry. As a result of the triumph of the Six-Day War, Jews today are proud of their ability to fight. This pride in physical reaction, missing from the Jewish body politic since the Judean-Roman Wars, sustains Israel today. Americans, Russians, Germans, Chinese: every nationality has pride in its military. So now does the Jewish people.

56

Star of David (Jewish Flag)

Symbols elicit pride in people. For Americans the sight of the Stars and Stripes provokes joy in God and country.

For Jews, their flag, with the Star (or shield) of David (Magen David) emblazoned in the middle against a white field delineated by two light blue lines, embodies God and country simultaneously. It is not only a secular symbol. It represents a history of struggle and has a resonance for Jews quite contrary to typical chauvinism.

The six-pointed star is an ancient symbol. Thought by the ancients to have magical and decorative significance, the Star of David is not countenanced by the Torah or Talmud. During the Middle Ages some Jewish mystics and kabbalists revered it for its supposedly magical powers. Perhaps its currency as a Jewish symbol was in response to the Christian cross. Although Jews in Prague (and later in Vienna and Amsterdam) appointed it as an official mark of the Jewish community, the Star of David has been used as a yellow badge for centuries to separate

Jews from gentiles. The Nazis, for example, insisted that Jews wear yellow stars at all times as badges of identification and "shame." Remarkably, a Jewish star was found by archeologists in the ruins of a third century Capernaum synagogue next to a pentagram—and a swastika.

Adopted by the Zionist movement at its first Congress in 1897 as the official symbol of the Jewish people, the Star of David was chosen in 1948 as the centerpiece of the blue and white flag of the State of Israel.

Although the menorah is thought by some to be the more authentic Jewish emblem, there is no easier way to bring forth Jewish pride than to raise our colors. The Star of David is the pulsing heart of the Jewish people.

57

Terezin (Theresienstadt)

In the medieval fortress town of Terezin, not far from the city of Prague in what is now the Czech Republic, Hitler "gave a city to the Jews." Theresienstadt (the German name for Terezin), known as the "model ghetto" to historians, was not really a city for Jews, and certainly not a place of refuge. The cafés, concert halls, schools, and hospitals the Germans showed to the Red Cross and the world could not disguise the fact that Theresienstadt was a *lager*, a concentration camp.

First used as an assembly point largely for German Jews (including highly decorated Jewish war veterans from the Austrian and German armies of World War I!) being transported to the death camps in the East (such as Auschwitz), Terezin was developed by the Nazi propagandists in an attempt to cover up their "Final Solution." Artists, writers, playwrights, and especially composers were allowed, for a brief time, to create and to produce their work for the inmate population. Despite the constant threat of deportation to sure death and horrid overcrowding, starvation, and disease, a flowering of artistry unparallelled in human history occurred, and all in a very short time.

From 1941 until 1945 Terezin was the home for composers Viktor Ullmann, Pavel Haas, Hans Krasa, and Gideon Klein; conductor Karel Ancerl; and the most prominent German rabbi (and a leading force in contemporary Judaism), Leo Baeck. The "paradise ghetto" was the home to instrumentalists from all the great European orchestras, from Vienna, Berlin, and Prague. The model "main street" was the home to dance bands like the Ghetto Swingers, to opera performed by children (Krasa's masterpiece, *Brundibar*), and to Verdi's *Requiem* performed by a chorus of famous singers accompanied by Klein (whom many compare now to Leonard Bernstein).

What remains of this Terezin are drawings by children of beautiful things and of death, of butterflies and the sky, of remembrances of life before incarceration and hunger. The production of Ullmann's *Emperor of Atlantis*, his sarcastic takeoff on this Nazi hell on earth, was halted by the Germans during its first dress rehearsal, all the players and its composer carted off to death in Auschwitz. Yet the opera and many of the works Ullmann's fellow composers created in Terezin survive. Their art is a proud testament of Jewish expression where daily survival was questionable but creativity somehow flourished.

58

Torah (As History)

A few questions and answers:

Q: Is the Torah history?

A: The Torah is a history. However, it is not a reference text in the way modern historians view history. The Torah is rather a history accepted by the Jewish people as their story (and a history of God, indeed "His Story"!).

Q: Did the events set forth in the Torah really happen?

A: The Torah is memory. There has been independent corroboration of many events in the Torah. However, so much of the Torah took place before recorded time that we can only guess whether it all was as it has been remembered.

Q: Are the times and dates set forth in the Torah historically correct?

A: The Torah is timeless. Unlike conventional histories, which often start at the beginning and go to the end, the Torah starts before time began and points us to when time will end.

Q: Are the portrayals of persons and places in the Torah historically accurate?

A: Abraham and Moses did exist. Abraham's birthplace has recently been excavated, and there is evidence in ancient Egyptian records that the Hebrews rebelled against their oppressors and fled into the Sinai. We have yet to locate Mount Sinai, although archeologists continue the quest.

Q: Was the Torah accepted by the Jewish people in ancient times as their "constitution"?

A: In 444 B.C.E., a public reading of the Torah was conducted in Jerusalem under the supervision of Ezra the Scribe.

Many view this as a public reaffirmation of the Sinai covenant. Others believe it was also the occasion of the completion of the written Torah in the form we know it today. The communal reading of the Torah on the Sabbath, and in traditional synagogues on Monday and Thursday, as well as on certain special holidays, has continued unabated for over 2,000 years.

Q: Why are Jews proud of the Torah?

A: The Torah was God's blueprint for the creation of the world. The Torah is for a Jew his natural place of being. Rabbi Akiba stated that without the Torah a Jew is like a fish out of water. Without water, a fish dies. Without Torah, a Jew is no more. Christians believe faith in their Christ supplants Torah. For Muslims, Torah is the basis of the Koran. The Torah is the most influential book in the history of humanity.

59

Warsaw Ghetto Uprising

There have been many heroic moments in Jewish history.

Yet the Warsaw Ghetto Uprising is unique because of when it took place and against whom it was waged. The German war against the Jews, known as the Holocaust to most, but more appropriately by the Hebrew word *Shoah*, was for many of its victims a period of utter futility and hopelessness. Indeed, the rebellion led by twenty-four-year-old Mordecai Anielewicz within the small confines of the Warsaw Ghetto was consciously fought with no chance of success. For the fighters, however, its very futility was the only justification they needed. Their message to the Germans and their National Socialism, to the Poles and their foolhardy anti-Semitism (the Polish underground refused to help in any material way), and to an uncaring world was that Jews could defy their annihilation with one machine gun, a handful of rifles and handguns, Molotov cocktails, and bricks, whatever it took. Not survival, necessarily, but RESISTANCE!

The ghetto was a small part of Warsaw closed off to pen in the city's Jews. At one point during the war it held over a half million Jews in the most horrid conditions. Those who did not die from starvation and exposure were eventually transported to death camps, the ghetto serving as a staging area and then an embarkation point to Auschwitz and the ovens.

By April of 1943 only sixty thousand Jews remained in the ghetto. They gathered the will to fight back, to stand up to the killers, despite their weakened physical state. When the Nazis marched in on the night of the first Passover Seder, the ghetto fighters struck back, killing German soldiers. The revolt lasted for twenty-seven days, longer than it had taken the German war machine to conquer all of Poland. The German soldiers were forced to level the ghetto building by building to still the flame of proud Jewish warriors.

The playwright William M. Hoffman has suggested that the retelling and analysis of the German war against the Jews since World War II is leading to the collective composition of a new section of the Bible—the Book of Shoah. Certainly in the bloody streets of the Warsaw Ghetto, its most compelling chapter, a source of Jewish pride for all time, was written by young men and women who would not lie down.

60

Western Wall

When the Israeli army recaptured East Jerusalem during the Six-Day War, one of the first people to arrive at the Western Wall was Gen. Moshe Dayan, the defense minister and one of the architects of Israel's victory. In time-honored tradition he slipped a piece of paper into the Wall's cracks, making a wish for his people and for peace.

The Western Wall is the holiest Jewish site. It is a massive structure that served as an outer wall around the Temple Mount and was the only wall remaining after the Romans destroyed the Temple during the Judean War in 70 C.E.

For centuries after the destruction of the Temple, small groups of Jews made their way to Israel, often at grave peril, to pray at the Wall. Their often plaintive cries for the restoration of the Temple and the return of the Jewish people to Zion prompted Arabs and Christians to dub it the Wailing Wall. Jews today are proud not to use the term Wailing Wall, but instead the Hebrew *Kotel ha-Ma-aravi* (or Western Wall).

The Israeli government has created a plaza before the Wall to accommodate the large number of the faithful who visit the Wall to conduct their prayers. It has become a well-regarded practice for bar mitzvahs and other important events (personal and state) to be conducted before the Wall. The preservation of this holy site and other edifices of religious significance (some only to Christians and Muslims) has national significance. Israel believes it is a matter of national pride to protect its locations of religious and historical importance.

61

Zionism

Zionism is the only "ism" (other than capitalism) to have survived the twentieth century.

Fascism and Communism are dead, yet the call to return to Zion is still heard clearly.

The roots of Zionism extend back to the Babylonian captivity in the sixth century B.C.E. and even further back to the wanderings of Abraham and his flock.

"The Lord your God shall bring you back from captivity . . . and gather you again from all the peoples . . . and bring you into the land which your fathers owned and you shall have it." (Deut. 30:1–5)

Zionism has a rich religious history. Jews of the Diaspora recited regularly in prayer for almost two thousand years their urgent desire to come back to Israel. It became a religious obligation to return to Zion.

Zionism stands today for two principles. First, that the autonomy and safety of the State of Israel must be guaranteed. Second, that all Jews have a right of return to the Jewish state (see Aliyah, topic number 33).

There are seemingly as many concepts of Zionism as what it means to be Jewish. Cultural, secular, religious, political, synthetic, and socialist forms of Zionism have been debated for over one hundred years.

The movement arose in reaction to the Czarist pogroms of the 1880s and out of personal visions such as Theodor Herzl's of an independent Jewish state, which he came to after witnessing the Dreyfus affair in France in the 1890s. Amid the squalor of the ghetto that was Eastern Europe during the late nineteenth century, some Orthodox rabbis recognized that the Jewish people had to establish the foundation *themselves* of the return to Zion. In an era of heightened nationalism, other more secular minds recognized that assimilating into European culture would fail to protect Jews from persecution. Only an independent state could provide the proper security for its people.

Whether Zionism developed out of a practical need for safety or from a religious imperative to return to the Holy Land (where all acts of living and dying were more sacred and closer to God's spirit), it has been an "ism" that has led to remarkable and positive results. The Jewish state is not only a modern miracle of spiritual renewal and a symbol of a liberated people, but a proud beacon of healing and redemption for the whole world.

PART III

CIVILIZATION

62

Aggadah

Much of Jewish writings consists of rules. Jewish law, or *halakhah* (see topic number 71) sets forth in legalisms how people should behave. The emphasis in Judaism on lawmaking and lawgiving might seem to restrict personal freedom. The rabbis over the centuries have asserted, however, that obeying its code of conduct sets us free.

Every Jewish writing other than the halakhah is called "aggadah." *Aggadah* means "narration." A good deal of the aggadah explains in everyday language why people should obey God's law. Through tales, folklore, sayings, stories, parables, metaphysics, and history, the aggadah clarifies for us the intent of the halakhah. One third of the Talmud is aggadah. The aggadah adds ethics and life to the halakhah, while the halakhah insures ethical conduct is followed.

The lessons of aggadic writing are never binding (unlike the law of the Torah, which must be strictly followed). The aggadot only reflect the personal opinions of individual authors. Whether their lessons are followed depends on the writers' authority over time and how effectively they set forth their particular expression.

Aggadic writing often reveals the influence of local cultures. Greek philosophy infuses much of the aggadah, showing the intimate and mutually beneficial relationship between the Hellenic and Jewish peoples over the centuries. Persian words from the Babylonian captivity also appear in the aggadah.

The aggadah is philosophy. The aggadah is theology. The aggadah is the clear and personal written voice of the Jewish people.

63

The Catskills

Dubbed the "Jewish Alps" by decades of entertainers, the Catskill Mountains in upstate New York were the summer resort of choice for countless American Jews from the 1920s until the Age of Aquarius (the 1960s). Other vacation sites in the United States and Canada were similar, but the Catskills represented vacationing on the grand scale. From small bungalow colonies to grand hotels in the Miami Beach style, the Catskills provided a comfortable and sometimes garishly luxurious respite from the harsh realities of city life. It seemed everyone fled the teeming cities (especially New York) during the hot and humid summer months to trade asphalt for grass, dull brown and gray shades for green and blue brilliance. The frenetic, sweaty rush to go to school or make a living in the tough and unforgiving metropolitan area was replaced by cozy naps in an Adirondack chair and "Simon Sez" games (a precursor perhaps of today's aerobics classes) led by a sarcastically loud social director.

Towns with picturesque names like Monticello, Liberty, and Falls-burg, and bodies of water straight out of Longfellow poetry, Lakes Kiamesha and Anawana, provided a quiet and cool respite from the Grand Concourse, Brownsville, and Flushing. The Parisians fled to the Riviera, the Greeks to their islands, and New York Jews went to "the mountains." You didn't have to say "Catskills." Everybody knew what you meant.

Many men sent their wives and children away for the whole summer. Band members, busboys, and bellhops were required by the owners of the hotels to entertain the often lonely women during the workweek (until their husbands came up for the weekend). Casual dancing sometimes led to more intimate encounters.

An entire entertainment industry was founded out of the often silly games played around the pool or on the lawn. Three generations of comedians and many actors honed their craft before live audiences raised on local theater and radio, who were not yet comfortable with television.

Eating in the Catskill hotels reached orgasmic heights (or depths, depending on your waistline). In Mal Z. Lawrence's famous words, a Mrs. Epstein's assertion that "I don't eat like this at home" was contrasted by the porter's plea to "Forklift the Epsteins!" when they checked out at the end of the summer. Jews who starved for centuries found a horn of plenty in their version of pioneer America.

The Catskills reminded immigrants of their rural roots, yet with a major difference—in upstate New York there were no pogroms led by Cossacks or Polish peasants. It was *our* vacation home. It was safe. Of course, Jewish hotels were open to all, and there were some Italian and German places that catered to their own. But mostly, the towns in Sullivan and Ulster counties catered to a Jewish clientele that reveled in the newly found bucolic settings and togetherness. For in the Catskill Mountains, Jews found their own American version of Eretz Yisrael—a place where almost everyone (except the "locals" who did stay apart, sometimes coldly) could be with everyone else, proud to be Jews in America on Jewish-owned land.

64

Chicken Soup

It is a big mistake to tell any Jewish mother that her chicken soup will not cure the common cold. "Of course, it will!" she will insist, pushing you into a chair for a heaping bowl of Jewish penicillin. "Enjoy!"

There is something comforting about Jewish food. Much Eastern European Jewish cooking may not be healthy for you ("high in cholesterol" is a euphemism), but it tastes so good. It is the original "Mom food." Perhaps it's one's memories of childhood—sitting at Seders with grandma and grandpa, or sharing Friday night dinners lit by only two candles—that make eating Jewish food so special and endearing.

There is, of course, really no one kind of Jewish cooking. The Diaspora assured that variety was the spice of Jewish eating. Jews adapted the cuisine of the countries they found themselves in, often adding newfangled Yiddish or Ladino names to dishes slightly different from the locals. Jews in Italy used the artichoke in their cooking, while those in Poland found the potato their vegetable of choice. Greeks baked with phyllo, while Russians prepared challah bread with eggs, yeast, water, and flour.

So what is so special about Jewish food?

Although its cuisine resembles the many countries of the Diaspora, almost every Jewish dish has deep religious and symbolic meaning. The Passover Seder table, for example, hosts a series of foods, each marked with metaphor. Unleavened bread, or matzo, to recall the hasty flight of the Israelites from Egypt; bitter herbs (*maror*) for harsh centuries in slavery; a roasted egg, a symbol of the holiday offering; a roasted shankbone in place of the Paschal lamb required by the Bible; and *charoset*, a paste of wine, apple, nuts, and cinnamon, a remembrance of the mortar from which the Israelites made bricks for their persecutors; all are powerful emblems of Passover. Dairy on Shavuot (strudels, cheese kreplach, blintzes, cheese knishes for the Ashkenazim and baklava in Sephardic tradition); poppyseed hamantashen ("Haman's hat") during Purim; potato pancakes, latkes, fried in oil at Hanukkah; and round challah loaves and apples dipped in honey at Rosh Hashanah are only some of the examples of food used to signify faith and memory.

For Jews eating is more than sustenance. While the body is being replenished, the lessons of Judaism and the history of a people are proudly declared.

65

Codes

Judaism is a religion firmly grounded and in many ways directed by its laws, or *halakhot* (see topic number 71). It is not enough for a Jew to believe in his religion. He or she must follow its tenets as well.

Halakhic rulings on almost every area of human behavior exist in the writings and rules of the sages. From the end of ancient times until this century, rabbis have expounded on issues of life and death, love and war, wealth and poverty, citizen and state. These decisions and regulations of the sages were historically weighed as to importance in direct relation to the fame and reputation of their issuer.

The need to have these rulings in one place became overwhelming. Over the centuries the halakhot were therefore compiled in great texts such as the *Mishnah* prepared by Judah the Prince (see topic number 14), the *Mishneh Torah* of Maimonides, and the *Shulhan Arukh* (or "set table" in English) of Joseph Caro.

The great responsibility of being Jewish—and a lifelong task—

would seem to be the study of these immense codes. Yet Rabbi Hillel (who lived a generation before Jesus of Nazareth and before the written codification of Jewish law) taught that the Golden Rule was all one needed to know, the rest being commentary.

Not leaving anything to chance, however, the sages since have felt it necessary to codify legal norms. Many of these rules guide the observant to proper behavior not only in religious practice but in everyday life. Religious practices—for worshipers in the ancient Temple in Jerusalem (see topic number 28) to those in Diaspora synagogues—participation in Sabbath and Festival observances, choice and preparation of Kosher food, sanitary procedures for menstruating women, counsel regarding giving, how to conduct funerals, the necessity of obeying one's parents, the correct way to give a brit (see topic number 3), rules of marriage and divorce, how to make a business contract, and how to litigate a case are all covered in depth in the Jewish codes.

Human behavior having changed little over the centuries, the Jewish codes provide a necessary source of reference and a civilizing force.

66

Comedians

It has been said that writing tragedy is so much easier than comedy. Making people laugh would appear to be a simpler task than making people cry. Yet, we remember the great tragedies of the Greeks and Shakespeare sooner than their comedies. Being a comic is more difficult than being an actor. Many comedians are great actors. How many great actors are also funny?

A disproportionate number of the great comedians of the past hundred years have been Jewish. The Marx Brothers, Jack Benny, George Burns (but not Gracie!), Bert Lahr, Milton Berle, Sid Caesar, Mel Brooks, Lenny Bruce, Woody Allen, Alan King, Jackie Mason, Joan Rivers, Jerry Seinfeld, and countless Buddys, Ziggys, Martys, Belles, and others share an inspiration in their religious background.

Jokes often seem only a step away from pain. "I laughed so much it hurt!" is a common refrain. Jews share with other long-suffering minority groups a particular affinity for lifting joy out of sorrow, laughter from tears. Only the great African-American comedians of recent vintage have tapped similar hysteria and strain.

Yet Jewish comedians have an almost Talmudic approach to making things appear funny. Set it up and then demolish it. Presentation and chaotic analysis. Rashi-like dissection of ideas and situations. Think of the spaceship in the opening sequence of Mel Brooks's *Spaceballs*. It appears across the blackness of space, filling the void with the roar of its engines and its battlements filling and filling and filling, over and over, again and again, with the relentlessness only Mel Brooks can serve up like an overflowing egg cream. And Sid Caesar "reading" hieroglyphics, Milton Berle sporting a floral dress with rouge makeup, Woody Allen turning into a Hasid at Granny Hall's table.

Out of the ghetto and shtetl came a shriek and a holler, a comedic righteousness, an attempt to gather all the broken pieces of the world and put them back together, only to shatter them apart (a reverse *tikkun*, see topic number 95). Jews have wept so much from the rivers of Babylon to the Blue Danube that laughing—and making other people laugh—has become their blessing for everyone.

67

Cruelty to Animals

Although there are many references in the Torah and Talmud to the ritual slaughter of animals, especially for Temple sacrifices, it is usually forgotten that the fourth of the Ten Commandments prohibits not only people from doing any work on the Sabbath but their beasts of burden from working as well. Indeed, so concerned are Jews about animals that the sanctity of Sabbath observance can be disturbed to rescue an animal from pain.

One of Judaism's greatest contributions to world civilization, and a source of great pride, is its emphasis on the prevention of cruelty to animals (in Hebrew, *tza'ar ba'alei khayyim*).

To this day Jews generally do not like to hunt. Perhaps having been hunted by bigots for thousands of years has given Jews a hatred for the chase.

Before man, most animals are defenseless. Jewish law indeed commands that animals be fed before sitting down to eat oneself. Farmers are urged to use animals of equal strength to pull their ploughs lest the weaker fall into the mud and be dragged.

Young birds or eggs must not be taken from the nest while the mother bird is present. Animals cannot be castrated. No cruelty of any kind is permissible. Indeed, the slaughter of animals for food must be done so swiftly that there is virtually no pain suffered, and death is instantaneous.

"A righteous man knows the needs of his beast." (Prov. 12:10)

68

Divorce

"For I hate divorce, says the Lord, the God of Israel." (Mal. 2:14–16)

To be unfaithful to one's spouse is viewed by the Torah as a traitorous act. The fidelity of the marital relationship has been treated by Jewish tradition as one of the core values of civilization.

Despite many abuses, divorce granted by religious authorities—the bill of divorcement, or *get*—is not readily available. The Talmud has lengthy regulations concerning the circumstances required before formal divorce will be granted. Sections in the Bible are most often cited in granting the husband, but not the wife, sole authority to seek divorce. In the tractate "Sanhedrin," the Talmud states that "the altar sheds tears for the man who divorces his first wife." In the Middle Ages, hundreds of years before modern feminism, the sages altered the Biblical method to require joint consent of both husband *and* wife.

A man has authority to divorce without the blessing of his wife. However, spouses will often seek the guidance of a rabbinical assembly called a *Bet Din* to resolve marital disputes. Certainly a woman needs the binding credibility of the Bet Din to divorce a husband.

Rabbinical courts are very reluctant to allow a man to give a *get* to his wife. The couple is brought before the court (sometimes the wife's failure to make her husband appear results in her living in a miserable half-state of marital disunion), interviewed, questioned, and urged to work out their problems. If such intervention fails to bring about reconciliation, and proper evidence and traditional legal requirements are fulfilled, then the bill of divorcement is permitted.

Pursuant to the Talmud, the courts can also legally *require* a husband to divorce his wife. If he refuses or fails to take care of her, denies her marital relations, beats her after being told to stop by rabbinical authorities, or contracts venereal disease, or if she fails to conceive a child by the tenth anniversary of marriage, divorce will be granted. Many of the fundamental principles of modern domestic-relations law and women's rights were first debated in rabbinical courts centuries ago when the rest of the world viewed wives as chattel to be exploited by their husbands in any way they desired.

69

Education

In the Shema, recited in the daily morning and evening prayers, Jews are required to make sure that biblical laws are imparted to their offspring.

"You shall teach them diligently to your children." (Deut. 6:7)

The Bible is rich in instructions not only to remember God's laws but to teach them to one's children from an early age. In several other places in Deuteronomy, and in the Books of Joshua, Proverbs, and Nehemiah, the Mishnah, and the Talmud, specific directions are set forth telling parents when and what portions of Jewish law are to be studied. These almost regulatory admonitions have unified Jewish learning with but a few regional differences.

Jews have been called the "people of the Book." This appellation is not far from the truth. During medieval times, when illiteracy among most of the population was rampant, the majority of Jewish men could read and many could debate the fine points of Jewish law. While many

Christian men of an intellectual bent went into the priesthood during this era, Jews established rabbinic dynasties. Learned scholars and teachers begat generations of educated men who enriched Jewish culture with their responses to and commentaries on questions of Jewish law and history.

With the change of Jewish faith from a stationary religion centered around the Temple in Jerusalem to a portable faith carried by the ideas of its followers, education of every male child became paramount. The establishment of the one-room class, or heder, and the Talmud school (yeshiva) modeled on the ancient Babylonian academy (see topic number 32, "Academies") coupled with a cultural obsession with literacy assured the survival of Judaism's values and the essence of its spiritual lessons.

70

Fiddlers on the Roof

It was thought to be the only way out of the ghetto. In today's inner cities in America, excellence in sports (especially basketball and boxing) is seen as an escape route from poverty. To impoverished young Russian Jews at the end of the nineteenth century and the beginning of the twentieth, becoming a violin virtuoso seemed like the best strategy to achieve freedom.

In the 1890s, a child prodigy, known to all by the nickname Mischa, played before the Czar. If little Mischa Elman could do it, reasoned parents across the Pale of the Settlement, so could "my Moishe" or "my Sasha" or "mein Totele." No reason why not. Little boys across Russia, and then across Europe and America, put on short pants and began to practice the violin.

Elman was followed by a progression of genius violin virtuosi, each eclipsing the previous. Efrem Zimbalist, Jascha Heifetz, and Nathan Milstein were all students of Leopold Auer, the Jewish founder of the great Russian string-playing tradition and a colleague of Tschaikovsky and Anton Rubinstein. All these violinists changed music, enriching our understanding of their instrument and its literature.

When Heifetz first performed to an enthusiastic audience at Carnegie Hall, the oft-repeated tale of the confrontation between Austrian Jewish violinist Fritz Kreisler and the pianist Leopold Godowsky occurred. Noticing that Kreisler was squirming in his seat during the Heifetz premiere, Godowsky asked if anything was wrong. Kreisler replied, "It's hot in here." Godowsky countered, "Not for pianists!"

Jewish dominance in playing stringed instruments was not limited to Russia. In addition to Auer's influence in Eastern Europe, Joseph Joachim, Brahms's dear friend and advisor, established a Germanic method of study that decidedly advanced the careers of Kreisler, Hubermann, and the Jews who participated in large numbers in Central European orchestras such as the Berlin and Czech Philharmonic prior to World War II.

After World War II the preeminent role of Jewish string players continued unabated with the flourishing careers of Yehudi Menuhin, Isaac Stern, Mstislav Rostropovich, Itzhak Perlman, Gidon Kremer, and Gil Shaham (as well as many others). The quivering tone of Jewish violinists and cellists since Auer seems to have risen up out of the suffering and hopes of centuries with an almost supernatural voice.

Their song provided the inspiration for Marc Chagall's image of a fiddler floating above the rooftops of snowy villages lifting lovers (and the rest of us) off the ground into everlasting bliss.

71

Halakhah

What is meant by *Jewish law*? Jewish law, *halakhah* in Hebrew, refers to the Written Law found in the Torah, especially in the Five Books of Moses (the Pentateuch) and the Oral Law. Halakhah has developed over the centuries reflecting the progress of the Jewish people through history and their understanding of divine law. The word *halakhah* comes from the Hebrew word for walking, an apt name, since the Law shows Jews the correct path to follow in their everyday lives.

To most religious Jews, halakhah and Torah are one and the same. Orthodox, Conservative, Reform, and Reconstructionist Jews differ on their view as to whether every word of the Torah has divine origin. It cannot be denied, however, that the Written Law as found in the Torah has a power unlike any other writing.

The Oral Law developed out of the human need to explain the Torah and its teachings clearly. From this need came the connection between generations we call tradition, as fathers taught sons and teachers instructed students in the lessons of Torah.

The method by which Torah was studied by the sages in ancient times is called Midrash (see topic number 13). It applied techniques of analysis aimed at bringing out the meanings of the Scripture and validating halakhah related through the Oral Law. The explanations, voluminous in number and often binding in their effect on everyday life, were assembled by Judah Ha-Nasi in the compendium called the "Mishnah" (see topic number 14). The commentaries on the Mishnah are, of course, known as the Talmud (see topic number 26).

In addition to the rules found in the Torah, further regulations (called *gizzard*) were instituted by rabbinical courts to ensure that God's commandments would not be violated. Additional edicts (*takkanot*) made the Law more flexible in responding to the changing mores of society over time. Local custom, or *minhag*, was also incorporated in halakhah to make the law responsive to regional needs. Finally, rabbis over the centuries have answered everyday questions from laypeople about the Law in what are known as Responsa, used to guide the perplexed to understanding.

Halakhah is remarkably flexible. Its very contemporary nature and ability to adapt to the modern technologic age has been dubbed eternal. It is the binding nature of halakhah that has kept the Jewish people together through the centuries and brought the highest possible standard of behavior to all of civilization.

72

Hebrew

Hebrew (*ivrit*) is the only modern tongue based on an ancient written language.

With origins in archaic Semitic dialects out of Canaan and Syria, and strongly showing the influence of Babylonian Aramaic, Hebrew has assumed idioms, expressions, and words from the host countries Jews found themselves in over the centuries. When Hebrew vocabulary was found to be wanting for scientific expression, Arabic was used in its stead, then borrowed to modify Hebrew into a more precise speech.

There have been three great ages of the Hebrew language.

Ancient Hebrew was developed first during the early years of a wandering people. Its relatively small treasury of words and its sentence structure were institutionalized during the reign of King Solomon. The use of Hebrew in ritual was gradually monopolized by the priests in the Temple in Jerusalem. After the Babylonian captivity, Aramaic became the common tongue of the Israelites, while Hebrew remained the language of prayer and priestly benedictions.

After the destruction of Judea by the Romans, Mishnaic Hebrew, a new language out of the old, evolved during the early years of the Diaspora. A common pronunciation throughout the dispersion of the Mishnah (see topic number 65, "Codes," and number 14, "Mishnah") affirmed this second stage of Hebrew. The language was further expanded by the introduction of words and patterns that could be used to describe familiar events. During the latter part of the Middle Ages, Hebrew was also used as the preferred language of scientific texts, its vocabulary of words having been expanded to meet new expectations.

Modern Hebrew was formulated by scholars (such as Eliezer ben-Yehuda and Shalom Ya'akov Abramovitch) to meet the demands of the industrial world and the settlement of Palestine. Hebrew was recommended to be the common language of all Jews, especially those inhabiting Israel. It was meant to be spoken not only in the synagogue (ancient Hebrew was still the language of most of the Torah), but also in the streets, in government offices, theaters, restaurants, and schools. The use of European languages and Yiddish was discouraged by the developers of modern Hebrew.

Their message urged pride in the use of our ancestors' language. Hebrew, they proudly held, had survived like the Jewish people. Although it had been marked by the centuries, it was now restored as the common tongue of a reunified nation.

73

Hollywood

The critic Neal Gabler has chronicled "how the Jews invented Hollywood" in his *An Empire of Their Own*. All the major studio heads, except Disney and Zanuck, who created the movie industry were Jewish. Mayer, Zukor, Laemmle, Cohn, Thalberg, Fox, Lasky, Schenck, Goldwyn, and the Warner brothers were some of the Jewish men who created the American motion-picture business. Many of the men and women who followed them were also Jews (from Selznick to Katzenberg). Hollywood has provided billions of people with a kind of mass entertainment unknown to prior generations of humanity.

The movies are often a form of escapism. Films meant to amuse or shock are frequently no more than froth or thrillers, passing fancies, fleeting images of celluloid. Yet the cinema (as Europeans are wont to call the movies) has changed the way we think and see. Telling a story through visual imagery, paintings come to life in movement, accompanied by swelling music inspiring the action, motion pictures (and its rich cousin television) are for many their only refuge and surest education.

Adapting literary and stage conventions to film, the early moviemakers reflected the social mores of their period in their creations: Mayer's homage to an America of apple pie and Andy Hardy; Laemmle's expressionist horror films of vampires (Jewish blood libel?) and Golem-like monsters; the Warners' gangster wars; and Thalberg's elegant costume dramas all provided a summary of the progress of the world according to these moguls. Largely for better (but sometimes, as in the blacklisting days of the McCarthy era, for much worse), they molded the cultural taste of whole populations of people, many of whom had never before had any access to artistic expressions. Strangely enough, this meltdown created an impulse for more thrills and chills, more sighing and weeping, greater cheers and jeers. It also related to a mass public a sense of morality, justice, and ethics. Despite the commercial intent of its creators, Hollywood became our home.

74

Hora

To dance is to move freely.

The most celebrated Jewish dance is the hora. Participants join hands or interlock arms and move (usually to the left) in a circle, stepping to the side, crossing legs over, then into the middle, pushing the ring inward and out, surrounding dancers in the center who are performing loving duets and solo leaps.

Derived from a Romanian folk dance, the hora has been made into an Israeli national pastime. During celebrations of good fortune, on holidays, and also as athletic recreation, this Jewish form of aerobics can be danced to both simple and complex step patterns. The popular song, "Hava Nagila," often accompanies hora dancing, but there are many more tunes, both traditional and contemporary, that rush people to the floor.

The rhythms of horas often mix sequences of two and three beats, propelling the pulses of the percussion and dancers' hearts. Men dance with women and with other men, women dance with women, it just depends on local customs of what is acceptable.

There are other traditional Jewish dances originating from countries throughout the Diaspora. Yet no other so dominates traditional Jewish dance as the hora. Jews dance it together, communally, not often in pairs or alone. A soloist performs for the enjoyment of those viewing his lunges and jumps.

The joyous (*freilich* in Yiddish) ring of people dancing the hora is a symbol of Jewish community and responsibility for each other. Jews dancing together celebrate with pride the freedom of living.

75

Idolatry

One of the greatest contributions of Judaism to world civilization was the ban on worshipping idols. "You shall have no other gods besides me. . . . You shall not make for yourself a graven image or any likeness of anything that is in the heaven above or on the earth below. . . . You shall not bow down to them or serve them." (The second of the Ten Commandments, Exod. 20:3–5)

The Torah requires that Jews die rather than commit murder or incest, or bow down to idols.

This prohibition on *avodah zarah* (foreign deification) was at first a reaction by the early Israelites to the idolatrous practices of their neighbors. The story of Abraham smashing the idols of his father, establishing monotheistic belief in one fell swoop, has resounded through the centuries. The Bible is, of course, rife with tales of the ancient Israelites disobeying God's edict (remember the Golden Calf) and being called to task for it by judges and prophets.

Muslims cherish their common fatherhood in Abraham; Islam shares Judaism's insistence on pure monotheistic worship. The Christian use of imagery, particularly in the statues and icons of the Catholic and Greek Orthodox churches and the belief in the Holy Trinity, has diluted or made its monotheism somewhat ambiguous (despite the chant of *credo in unum Deum*).

The restriction on the creation of graven images, while acting as a stabilizing force in civilization, restrained Jews from participating in the fine arts until very recently. There is no Jewish El Greco or Rembrandt. Jews did not paint the Sistine Chapel or the Mona Lisa. Not until the past century did Jews (Pissarro, Chagall, Modigliani, Man Ray, Rothko) find expression in drawn or sculpted imagery.

Despite the inhibiting effect of the Second Commandment on Jewish artistic expression, this denial of idolatry led the world away from bestial practices. If one is forced to pray to something abstract, not of this world, not in the form of a hawk or a reptile, but of a force unknowable and greater than anything, then perhaps a looking inward, rather than to the outer world, will take place, taming the beast inside all of us.

76

Jewish Guilt

Where does "Jewish guilt" come from? Is there something Jews have to feel guilty about more than any other people?

When God directed the Jewish people to be a "light unto the nations," a weighty responsibility was laid on His Chosen People. The ancient Israelites were hardly consistently righteous. The Bible is rich in descriptions of their transgressions. The ancients were people after all, not just archetypes. Their human foibles still compel us to read the Scriptures as if they were today's unfolding melodrama or yesterday's news. They shouted, wept, smiled, and worried like other human beings. The modern intoxication with the story of Genesis is but one example of our continuing fascination.

But the ancients—and their descendants—were followers of a religion that has never been finished. There is no final and absolute way to be a Jew. The Jewish people have fussed over their beliefs for thousands of years. They have waged a battle for their own souls happily lost in the doing, but won, most often, for the trying.

This sense of responsibility and compulsion for order and truth have inspired Jewry to compose rules of behavior and then commentaries on these regulations, commentaries on commentaries on the regulations, in what seems like a never-ending circle, and the extrapolation of new rules out of the old. So many rules, some non-Jews have wondered, why bother? The Jewish answer has been that it is our worrying over how we do things in our search for God that has enriched all of humanity.

Perhaps the Nazi hatred of the Jews arose not only from the corrupt need for an age-old scapegoat, but out of hysterical fear that Judaic concern for all life (the example of Torah and Talmud and their powerful claim on civilization) shone too bright a light on their evil path. Today it often seems that the world holds Israeli political action to a different and higher standard than that of any other country. It is not just about oil and the money that flows from it.

Over the centuries, Jews' guilt about the state of themselves and their world has led to equal portions of accomplishment and suffering. When the world worries as much about the state of the Jewish people, our common civilization will seem like paradise.

77

Jewish Mother

Before there was Jewish guilt, there was the Jewish mother.

Much maligned by Catskill comedians, reviled by contemporary novelists, feared and beloved by Jewish children, the figure of the mother looms immense in Judaic history and home life. Until the founder of Hadassah, Henrietta Szold, and Israeli political leader Golda Meir in modern times, Jewish women, and especially Jewish mothers, played a subservient public role. Not until the 1960s were Jewish females even allowed near the Torah in Conservative synagogues. Women are still separated from men in Orthodox congregations and cannot approach the sacred scrolls.

Yet in their homes, among their families, Jewish mothers have had, especially in Ashkenazic communities, a predominant position. Prior to their social emancipation in America and Europe, Jewish women were expected by tradition to cater to their husbands, bear their children, obey their commands, and expect little from life other than satisfaction in the growth and safety of their families.

Jewish biblical history seems fashioned from the whims and desires of the great Patriarchs. Yet as recent examinations of Genesis in particular have shown, the Patriarchs often acted on the direction or innuendo of their wives and mothers. Sarah, Rachel, Rebecca, and Leah in many ways "ruled the roost."

Jewish mothers can even play favorites. Sarah manipulated Abraham to conceive a son, Ishmael, with her slave girl Hagar, only to cast them out when by miracle she gave birth to their only son together, Isaac. A generation later, with the help of their mother, Rebeccah, Jacob cheated his brother Esau out of his inheritance from Isaac.

The Jewish mother is perhaps no different, at least outwardly, from, for example, the Chinese or Hispanic mother. All mothers would seem to be the same, to care the same. To think otherwise would seem to be a kind of prejudice.

However, Jewish mothers guided their children to the behavior that changed the world. When their husbands and children acted apart from Hebraic values, Jewish mothers reined them in. With an aggression only exceeded by their caring, they brought an intensity to their love for their children that has proven to be as overwhelming as it is enlightening.

78

Kabbalah

Mystics throughout the ages have sought alternative ways to reach God. Traditional prayers and services have never been enough for those who seek the hidden meaning behind everything.

Some have viewed their mystical ideas as more important or as a replacement for custom. Indeed, the name of the Jewish mystical movement that originated in the late twelfth century called itself Kabbalah (tradition) in Hebrew.

Jewish mysticism has its roots in ancient times. The *Hekhalot* mysteries are attributed to the time of Rabbi Akiba, just before the final destruction of the Judean kingdom by the Romans during the Bar Kokhba revolt of 135 C.E. These mysteries are visions of God's realm detailing the paths of His celestial kingdom.

The hidden, eternal truth was not always attempted by Jewish mystics solely through visions, dreams, and prophecy. Through a highly developed system of symbols and numerology, kabbalists in the thirteenth century attempted to find a way to reveal what words cannot say and thoughts will not express. These mystics did not trust that words alone could fully impart the spirit of God.

The Torah is viewed by Jewish mystics as a kind of guidebook of symbols waiting to be uncovered, their deepest meanings exposed. The kabbalists used an elaborate system of numbers to try to make sense of the unknowable. They felt that what words could not express, numbers might.

Jewish mystics generally studied in small groups away from mainstream religious practices. Composition of the *Zohar*, the principal texts of Jewish mysticism in Spain during the late thirteenth century, and the work of Isaac Luria's circle of kabbalists in Safed during the sixteenth century were accomplished largely in secret.

By the late seventeenth century the secrets of ancient Jewish mysticism had been politicized. Jewish mysticism had developed into an almost hysterical messianism resulting in mass movements centered around the so-called False Messiah, Shabbetai Tzvi. The emphasis on finding the truth behind sacred words shifted to searching for a leader who would redeem our sins on Earth—a Messiah. Messianism, derived from kabbalistic teachings, gave persecuted Jews of the late Middle Ages hope and a powerful inspiration to force their way out of the ghetto.

Kabbalah remains a potent force. Jews are not only a people of the Book. The redemption of the Jewish people lies as well in the symbols God has left us in scripture and ancient manuscripts.

79

Ketubbah

The *ketubbah*, or marriage contract, sets forth the rights of a husband toward his wife. Signed by the couple before the marriage ceremony, the ketubbah establishes the mostly financial responsibilities a man must show his wife after the wedding. The content of the ketubbah has been thought to have such paramount importance as to receive the attention of some of the greatest religious minds in Jewish history. Both Torah and Talmud have detailed provisions regulating the marriage act as signified by the ketubbah. During the Middle Ages Maimonides set forth his own view of these obligations in his code, the *Mishneh Torah*, and Joseph Caro, the great codifier of Jewish law, did the same in his magnum opus, the *Shulkhan Arukh*.

Although traditionally ketubbot have been written in Aramaic, the common language of ancient Judea, there is a trend in modern times for Hebrew and/or a local language to be used in addition or even substitution. The statements found in the ketubbah are so important as to demand the almost instant communication only registered by every-day speech.

The ketubbah is one of the few items of Jewish religious practice to be visually beautiful. Since the Middle Ages, ketubbot have been illuminated with elaborate design and bright colors. These ornate contracts virtually woo the bride into execution.

A conventional prenuptial agreement spells out what happens when a couple separates or divorces. The ketubbah directs, particularly the man, how the couple must act contractually with each other in their household. Seen as a legal microcosm of the world of marital affairs, the ketubbah acts as a regulatory mean for all Jewish couples to follow. Especially in the home, the seat of our common civilization, Jewish law guides the family in the duties of the marital union.

80

Kibbutz

The Jews who settled in Palestine at the beginning of the twentieth century thought of themselves as pioneers. Most of them had fled from
Czarist repression, trading the cold steppes of Russia for the arid sand
of the Negev. In the Old Country, few had been farmers. None had ever
owned land. However, they knew that to change Palestine into the land
of Israel, it was required that they till the soil, learn how to grow crops,
change deserts into orchards.

Few felt that this could be accomplished alone.

Drawing on idealistic models such as utopian communities and
socialism, the early settlers banded together and shared the responsibility and the benefits of communal ownership. In 1910 the first kibbutz, a cooperative farming settlement, was started in a town called
Degania (the first baby to be born there was Moshe Dayan, the future
war hero, general, defense minister, and legend).

Today there are varied kinds of kibbutzim. In the traditional kibbutz, everything is shared. Children live together in a children's house, all property is owned, and all work organized on a collective basis. In theory, members of a kibbutz produce according to their individual talents and in turn receive housing, food, clothing, and medical services corresponding to their needs. Many kibbutzim are quite successful. Most are governed by a central committee elected by the members. The traditional kibbutz may be the only true success story of socialism. Other types of kibbutzim promote religious precepts, such as mixing Torah with threshing, while the remainder are more secular or political.

Most people do not realize that less than five percent of the entire Israeli population lives on a kibbutz. Yet the kibbutz has become identified with the "idea" of a resilient State of Israel, that idea being that together "kibbutzniks" can meet any challenge.

81

Klezmer Music

The wail of a high-pitched clarinet, a "zetz" on the drum, the "oompah-pah" of the tuba, a plaintive melody yanking memories of the shtetl out of the air: Sounds of *klezmorim* (traditionally, musicians playing Eastern European folk music) make forgotten village life instantly real.

Like Yiddish, which many say is a dying language with more lives than a cat, klezmer music is alive and well. Young musicians throughout the United States, Europe, and Israel have discovered its vibrant rhythms, surging, expressive themes, and poignant lyrics. Not just a nostalgic art, klezmer music is being composed today. When coupled with virtuoso performers like Itzhak Perlman, klezmer sells out Radio City Music Hall in New York. In Poland, where only a few thousand Jews remain from a pre–World War II population of three million, klezmer festivals are joyously attended by young Polish audiences, dancing about to klezmer music played by Polish performers, not a Jew among them.

Klezmer is Yiddish jazz. Like jazz, it is the music of a people and in some ways is their history. Originally dance music, it is now most often heard in the concert hall. A people's music, not of the conservatory, klezmer is about everyday things, yet has its visionary side. Its *freilachs*, whirling insistent tunes, rush up and toss you onto the dance floor, heart beating, to make it into the circle of dancers. Horas, mazurkas, kazatskas, waltzes, and marches, are all basic and elemental dances and the staples of klezmer music. It is the ballet of the People, once lost in the Diaspora with no hope of escape, rushing about, arm in arm, freed by klezmer's liberating force.

82

Ladino

Judeo-Spanish, Solitreo, Judezmo, and Judeo-Español are names for the traditional language of the Sephardim most commonly called "Ladino." After their expulsion from Spain in 1492, Sephardic Jews throughout the Balkans, Turkey, and North Africa talked to each other in a tongue derived from medieval Spanish that incorporated the dialects of the areas they settled in. Bits of English, Greek, Turkish, French, and Arabic combined to give Ladino its unique vocabulary and timbre.

Until the middle of the twentieth century, Ladino was the collective means of expression for Sephardim. Although the pronunciation of certain words and phrases might differ between a Bosnian Jew and his Italian cousin, fundamental Ladino was comprehended by all Sephardic Jews. It served as the foundation of Sephardic society and the language of their commerce and culture.

Ladino was also used in translating countless Hebrew texts. Due to this translation of an immense literature, many ancient Hebrew scrolls that might have been lost were preserved.

Similar to the erosion of Yiddish as an everyday language, the number of Ladino speakers has been steadily decreasing. The Sephardic communities of Greece and of the Balkans suffered horribly during the Shoah (over 90 percent of Greek Jewry was destroyed). Sephardic Jews who emigrated to Israel, France, or the United States adopted the vernacular of the lands in which they settled.

However, despite the shrinkage of Ladino-speaking people, the Sephardic pronunciation of Hebrew became, first in Israel and then in the rest of the world, acceptable and then the norm. Sephardic songs with Ladino texts with their unique flavor and character remain at the spiritual core of Jewish expression.

83

Life

When Jews lift their glasses of wine in toast, they shout (as made famous in *Fiddler on the Roof*) "l'chaim!"—not "cheers!" or "bottoms up!", but "to life!"

Life is the most blessed value in all of Jewish thought. Power, wealth, and success are all meaningless before what truly and only counts—life. Life is so precious because it comes directly from God. Jews view life as God's gift.

The image of the tree of life reaching to the heavens is forever embedded in the Jewish psyche. Life must be sustained not only from the earth's bounty, but also by God's commandments on high. Yet if life is threatened, Jews are directed (there is no argument!) to break any of those commandments, including desecrating the Sabbath (but never under any circumstances, to worship idols, spill blood, or engage in sexual perversity). To save a life is to save the world.

When God stopped Abraham from sacrificing Isaac, the world was taught a lesson. Not only human sacrifice is forbidden. There is no civilization when people kill each other. The Jewish conception of the preservation of life extends to the tender love parents are required to give to their children, to the holiness of marriage, and to the stability and fairness of good government.

Jews should be immeasurably proud that Jewish love of life is the foundation of all civilized living.

84

Lower East Side

Whenever Jews emigrated to a new country, they initially tended like other ethnic groups, to settle together in one area. In countries where human rights were denied, these areas often became ghettos. In America, the most prominent place Jewish immigrants first settled was the section of New York City known as the Lower East Side.

Essex, Hester, Ludlow, Rivington, Orchard, Delancey, Grand, and Broome are names of streets that for all time will be an essential part of Jewish civilization. This pavement among tenements and retail shops symbolizes the early life of Jewish immigrants in America, when the slow pace of the villages of Eastern Europe was replaced with the furious pace of the Lower East Side of Manhattan. Like Krochmalna Street in the Warsaw of author Isaac Bashevis Singer's youth or Dizengoff Street in today's Tel Aviv, the Lower East Side became the center of Jewish life in the New World.

At the turn of the twentieth century the Lower East Side had more people than places for them to sleep. Conditions were horrendous. Families of eight and more were squeezed into squalid apartments of three rooms or less. Few apartments had proper, let alone, private, sanitary facilities.

Parents eked out the bare necessities for their children doing "piece work" for the garment industry, often at home. In the days prior to child labor laws and organized unions, working conditions in so-called sweatshops contributed to disease and the affliction of unrelenting, abysmally hard labor. The price of freedom and opportunity in America was sometimes brutal working conditions reminiscent of the plight of Israelite slaves among the pyramids of Egypt.

Out of these hard times came a good portion of modern American Jewry. Their forebears' inordinate sacrifice and courage should always signify more than nostalgia. The example of these immigrants was about more than hard work in impossible working conditions. Many of the social benefits granted to workers in the clothing industries today were first conceived and won by laborers as a result of their experiences on the Lower East Side. Yiddish theater had a renaissance in America on New York's Second Avenue, with stars such as Maurice Schwartz, Boris Tomashevsky, Menashe Skulnik, and Molly Picon paving the way for Paul Muni, Edward G. Robinson, and Lee Strasberg (and the generations of "method" actors who followed).

Today the Lower East Side is a bargain hunter's paradise with shops along Orchard Street discounting uptown sale prices of name-brand merchandise. Pickles can still be purchased from big barrels filled with brine. The area retains the echoes of immigrants shuffling their wares across crowded streets, the unique smells of Kosher kitchens, and the noise of thousands of souls finding their way into America.

85

Maccabbiah

Since 1932 in Tel Aviv, Jewish athletes from all over the world have competed in the Maccabbiah Games. Today, over six thousand athletes from fifty countries compete in over forty different sports.

The stated purpose of the Maccabbiah Games has always been to encourage Jewish youths to celebrate their background and to promote physical fitness. In a remarkable show of athletic (and Jewish) pride, competitors in the Maccabbiah pursue competition in games sanctioned by the International Olympic Committee.

The Maccabbiah grew out of Jewish pride.

At the end of the nineteenth century, young Zionists, passionately committed to the establishment of a Jewish state in Palestine, recognized the necessity of physical training. Responding to this desire, gymnastic clubs were opened in Jewish communities across Central and Eastern Europe. Zionist leaders such as Max Nordau insisted that Jews develop muscle in concert with their spiritual and ethical values.

Nordau urged that "the more Jews achieve in the various branches of sport, the greater will be their self-confidence and self-respect." Stirred on by the Maccabbi World Union, the official organizing entity of the Maccabbiah, Jewish sports activities were organized in the late 1920s out of Berlin. Just before World War II the union had a membership of over two hundred thousand athletes. After the Holocaust and the destruction of many of the nascent Maccabbi groups, new clubs were founded in the Americas and, most prominently, in Israel.

The Jewish Olympics, the Maccabbiah, has heightened the expectations of Jewish athletes worldwide. The gymnastic clubs from which it grew, and the growing Jewish awareness of physical fitness and team sports, prepared the way for the athleticism of trail-blazing sports heroes in track and field, baseball, boxing, football, and basketball. Pride in one's muscular development—and the groundbreaking work of the Maccabbi World Union—led directly to the conditioning of the Haganah, Israel's defense forces, and the rugged life of the kibbutz.

A sound mind can learn Talmud while working out to achieve a sound body.

86

Mikvah

For many Jews today, the *mikvah*, or ritual bath, is an archaic custom. To immerse oneself wholly in a public bath for purely religious reasons is an act of faith that many Jews, especially Reform Jews, refuse to make. To the contrary, Conservative Judaism officially respects the practice while Orthodox Jews view the mikvah as a basic component of their religious pride.

Since ancient times, the mikvah has been a fundamental element of Jewish life. A mikvah was found in every town along with a synagogue and religious school. Trips to the Temple in Jerusalem were forbidden without a prior visit to the mikvah. Detailed rules for its construction and directives about its usage were debated and set forth by the great scholars in the Talmud and in rabbinical literature. The mikvah is one of the few surviving practices of the Temple period. It has lasted the two thousand years since the destruction of the Temple due to careful observance by the righteous and because of its deeply symbolic and religious meaning.

One does not "take a bath" in the mikvah. Indeed, one must take a separate shower or bath and be sparkling clean before going to the mikvah. The mikvah is a *ritual* bath. A specified quantity of water collected from underground springwater or collected from rain, snow, and ice is meant to cleanse solely in the spiritual sense. The Bible is clear in its statement that "only a spring, cistern, or collection of waters shall be cleansing" (Lev. 11:36).

What needs to be cleaned is any contact with aspects of life and death deemed by religious law to be impure. Sources of contamination include a woman's menstrual period, birth of a child, sexually transmitted diseases, ejaculation of semen, and contact with the dead.

Judaism's identification of these matters as impurities necessitating ritual cleansing may seem unsettling to contemporary readers. Yet the requirements of the mikvah have had a civilizing purpose. Touching upon the most intimate matters of the creation of life and the tending of its result in death, Jews are called naked before God to purify their physiques. Indeed, many very religious Jews view going to the mikvah as so important that they visit it prior to every Sabbath as well as before Yom Kippur. Surely a cleansed spirit will follow a purified body.

87

Minority Rights

Jewish tradition has always stressed a concern for those in need. This historical consideration for those less fortunate has expanded in modern times into a dynamic role in the protection of minority rights.

No other group has given so much of itself to the cause of civil rights (both financially and with its life's blood) as Jews in the United States (and to some extent those in South Africa, England, and South America). Some prominent examples come to mind immediately. During the early years of the civil rights struggle in America during the 1950s and 1960s, half the funding of African-American organizations came from Jewish sources. Two of the presidents of the NAACP have been Jewish. Two Jews, Andrew Goodman and Michael Schwerner, were slain in Mississippi in the early 1960s for their support of racial equality. During the 1990s, Jewish groups, such as the American Jewish Committee, raised money to rebuild Black churches in Southern communities torched by the fires of hate. Outside of the United States, in South Africa, Helen Suzman, a Jewish politician, aided Nelson Mandela and his African National Congress during their difficult uphill fight against apartheid.

Black-Jewish relations have suffered with the rise of African nationalism, its sometime-alignment (until recently)with Palestinian terrorists, and Black Muslim anti-Semitism. Differing philosophies on quotas and affirmative action have also polarized Jewish relations with African Americans to some extent. Yet despite two decades of tension, Jewish participation in issues of minority representation in our society and belief in the ethical necessity of equal opportunity for all continues with remarkable vigor and passion.

Opponents of Jewish support for minority rights have cynically claimed that it is based in Judaism's fears about self-preservation. If this were true, then Jews would have aligned themselves with the majority who kept silent and did nothing during the early years of the civil rights movement. Instead, Jewish men and women put their lives literally on the line, defending those whom others would hate simply because they were somehow different. Jews have a unique empathy for what the philosopher Martin Buber called "Other."

88

Mitzvot

Most people know right from wrong. We are supposed to learn what is good and what is evil from our parents. Indeed, Jewish law mandates that a father teach his children correct behavior from their earliest years so that when a girl reaches twelve and a boy thirteen, each is a responsible human being.

Judaism mandates that Jews follow God's commandments as a religious duty. Six hundred thirteen commandments are listed by tradition as a starting point. Yet the sages have noted that any commendable deed is a blessing. These acts of righteousness are called *mitzvot* in Hebrew (singular, *mitzvah*).

The obligation to perform mitzvot resulted in the Jewish obligation to work toward the perfection of humanity, what has become a refinement process. People have to be told how to control their instincts, make the proper choices, and get along with one another. Maimonides viewed mitzvot as not having been given randomly, but to help us. Contemporary thinkers like Joseph D. Soloveichik see mitzvot as not only controls on instinctual conduct but as impetus for everyone to think about when doing something or making a conscious choice.

Simply to perform mitzvot without any recognition of what good is being done is insufficient. This awareness, called *kavanah*, insures man's recognition that God's laws are being obeyed. Even if mitzvot are not performed wholly, it is fine, just so long as they are attempted. The rabbis have even held that one can do mitzvot with a hidden motive ("if I do this good deed, I'll get something as a result"). Next time one may do the mitzvot for the satisfaction of doing them for themselves and for nothing else.

Jewish tradition and history have varied answers as to whether performing mitzvot brings rewards. While the Torah guarantees peace and good fortune, rabbis over the centuries have debated over whether mitzvot produce any honors. To be sure, mitzvot redeem our lives. There is no greater joy than performing deeds judged worthy of God.

89

Organizations

Accomplishing what you set out to do can often only occur if someone gives you help. With assistance, you can get done what you sought to achieve.

Jewish tradition requires Jews to help each other. This custom of sharing our common fate comes not only from Scripture, but also from centuries of life in nations often hostile to their Jews. Even before the rise in the late nineteenth and early twentieth centuries of major Jewish charitable and political organizations, Jews banded together in the villages of Eastern Europe and in the Sephardic communities of Africa and the Middle East to aid the poor and run their own affairs.

It would seem that there was little need for such organizations in the United States. American concern for human rights and constitutional freedoms would appear to mute the desire to form organizations to protect Jewish interests. It is a mark of the importance of Jewish concern for the sharing of responsibility that despite this the growth of such organizations has developed to a much larger scale in America.

There is no shortage in the United States of powerful and committed organized Jewish groups. The American Jewish Committee, United Jewish Appeal, Workmen's Circle, YIVO, Anti-Defamation League, World Jewish Congress, Hadassah, and Chabad Lubavitch are only a few examples of the dozens of Jewish organizations helping Jews live better lives.

Unlike their historical predecessors in the small villages of the Diaspora, these American organizations (and their counterparts outside of the United States such as Jewish Care in England) help not only Jews but people of every background.

The stated purpose of these organizations is essentially communal. Their organized attention to sharing responsibility and making sure we all *care* perpetuates not only traditional Jewish notions of charity but also our pride in knowing that we have made a difference during our time on Earth.

90

Scientific Boxing

Jews are not thought of as athletes. The stereotype of the Jew to the anti-Semite is someone out of shape, wearing a kippah over an ill-fitting dusty black suit.

Yet before Muhammed Ali, Sugar Ray Robinson, and Joe Louis, Benny Leonard, a Jewish fighter, developed what has become known in modern times as "scientific boxing" (and one hundred twenty-five years before, in late eighteenth-century England, a Sephardic Jew named Daniel Mendoza first applied and then taught the skills later developed by Leonard). Bobbing and weaving, not just manhandling your opponent with unthinking brawn; and skillful jabs, crosses, and uppercuts, not wild, strong punches, are some of the techniques used by the boxer. Boxers wear down an adversary, they don't take him out with one punch.

"He's a great boxer" means that he is a great athlete. Not just a fighter or puncher, the boxer knows how to use the ring to his advantage. Like Michael Jordan, always knowledgeable of the movement of his teammates across the court, or Ty Cobb, laying down a bunt that his opponents cannot reach in time, the boxer always has a sense of the fight's boundaries. In that sphere the boxer seeks to control the maneuvers of his competitor, utilizing his boxing ability, not just his punching power, to carve victory out of his opponent's flesh.

The influence of Mendoza and Leonard on boxing history is overwhelming. Their example proved that Jews, so often the punching bag of bigots, could use their brains and quick hands to be the last standing at the sound of the bell.

91

Shalom

Most people want to live in peace with one another. However, no people has so much wanted peace as the Jews and had so little of it.

From their very beginnings as a nomadic people under a restless Abraham, through the early Kingdoms, the exile in Babylonia, the Hasmonean restoration, the Judean Wars, the Diaspora, the Inquisition, pogroms, the Shoah, and the creation of the State of Israel, Jews have seemingly been under fire from much of the Western World.

The great Nazi hunter Simon Wiesenthal has assembled a time line of persecution against world Jewry, and it is remarkable for its list of tales of hate and degradation over the centuries in almost every country in Europe, the Americas, and the Middle East. Before the blood libel reared its ugly head in Czarist Russia during the late 1800s, Jews had been slaughtered in twelfth-century England for their supposed ritual slaying of a boy, Hugh of Lincoln (Appalachian folk songs still bemoan his death). Centuries before Hitler fashioned what he hoped was the extermination of world Jewry through mechanized warfare, the Protestant reformer Martin Luther called for all Jews to be burned.

Judaism is a religion that fosters civilized behavior. Evil cannot exist in civilization, and it seeks out the civilized for destruction.

We all know of mankind's inhumanity, the almost insatiable desire to inflict harm on those less fortunate or weaker; the scapegoating of people not like ourselves. No other group in world history has been at the receiving end of so much hatred as the Jewish people. Yet what has been the Jewish response?

When other people of other nationalities greet each other, they say "Good day," "How are you?," "Hello!," "Nice to see you," or "Hi!" The Jewish greeting for thousands of years has been "Shalom," or its longer form, "Shalom aleichem" ("salaam aleikhem" in Arabic). "Peace" or "Peace be unto you" is wholly different than welcoming someone. Jews do not greet each other with the word "Violence" or the phrase "I am going to beat you up!"

Saying "shalom" carries with it a responsibility. It is not just a casual salute. If you hear "Shalom aleichem" said to you, you respond turning the phrase around, completing the circle, "Aleichem shalom" ("Unto you peace"). We meet in the desert of our lives acknowledging that there is only civilization if we grant each other peace.

SHALOM!

92

Shtetl

Many of our grandparents frequently asked of each other, "Where are you from?"

Many Jews in the Americas, Western Europe, and Israel can answer for their forebears that they are originally from some small village in a forgotten corner of Eastern Europe. The Pale of the Settlement, the Czarist demarcated enclave where Jews were permitted to live in Russia and parts of what is now Poland contained most of these *shtetlach* (Yiddish for "villages," the singular is *shtetl*).

Many of us have a nostalgic view of life in the shtetl, mostly encouraged by Marc Chagall's paintings and Tevye's Anatevka in the musical *Fiddler on the Roof*, which was inspired by the writings of Sholem Aleichem, the Jewish Mark Twain.

Yet life in the shtetl was for centuries miserable. Not much different from Christian villages of their day, shtetlach had poor sanitary conditions, dilapidated housing, and high rates of child mortality.

How shtetls were strikingly different from their contemporaries, however, was their emphasis on prayer and study. While most of Europe remained illiterate (except for monastic scholars), Jews formed little Jerusalems all over their region. The Temple may have been destroyed by the Romans (as had sanctuaries of countless other cultures), but the poor villagers of Eastern Europe clung to ancient custom, ritual, and learning in study houses and small synagogues.

There was no lack of desire to probe the lessons of thousands of years of civilization and to preserve order in the midst of medieval chaos. Shtetl dwellers organized their lives as best as they could following the dictates not simply of local rulers but, more important, of Jewish law. Burial societies were initiated, cheders (religious schools) opened to educate the young in Judaism, animals slaughtered by "shohets" (ritual butchers), and charities set up to help the destitute.

The chant of "next year in Jerusalem" was heard throughout the shtetl on holidays and on Shabbat, a reminder that Jewish civilization had a purpose and had to be preserved in now almost forgotten villages throughout the fields and mountains of Eastern Europe.

93

Song of Songs

"There is nothing in all the world quite like the day when the Song of Songs was given to Israel, for all its writings are holy, but the Song of Songs is its most holy." (Rabbi Akiva, second century)

The Song of Songs (also called the Song of Solomon) is an anthology of love poems. Quite unlike any other text in the Scriptures, the Song of Songs does not mention God (the Book of Esther, the Megillah, also shares this rather special credential). Its imagery revels in the pleasures of secular, not religious, allusion. Valleys, flowers, perfumes, breasts, wild animals, tents, oils, wine, rocks, and vineyards provide some of its elaborately poetic metaphors.

The Song of Songs does not tell a story. It makes no judgments. For the rabbis, its inclusion in the canon of Biblical writings was confirmed only when the lover was identified as God and the Beloved as the congregation of Israel. For writers, it is a model of intricate style and poetic grace.

Chanted in the synagogue on the Sabbath during Passover (and by the Sephardim after their Seder), the Song of Songs is a celebration of life. The bride sings, the lovers speak intimately, the woman remembers her love, a wedding is celebrated, a youth croons of his love's beauty, the bridegroom is sought, passion blooms in a vineyard, lovers unite like brother and sister. Although short in number of verses, the Song of Songs is a treasury of literary effects, of the creative urge.

If the sages who amassed the writings constituting the Scriptures had not included it, the Song of Songs would most likely have been forgotten. Its special meaning to these great scholars and the observant (and to creators and lovers since) insured its primacy in the use of loving words.

ו אָנָה הָלַךְ דּוֹדֵךְ הַיָּפָה בַּנָּשִׁים
אָנָה פָּנָה דוֹדֵךְ וּנְבַקְשֶׁנּוּ עִמָּךְ:

דּוֹדִי

יָרַד לְגַנּוֹ לַעֲרוּגוֹת הַבֹּשֶׂם לִרְעוֹת בַּגַּנִּים
וְלִלְקֹט שׁוֹשַׁנִּים:

אֲנִי לְדוֹדִי וְדוֹדִי

לִי הָרוֹעֶה בַּשׁוֹשַׁנִּים:

'Whither is thy beloved gone,
O thou fairest among women?
Whither hath thy beloved turned him,
That we may seek him with thee?'
'My beloved is gone down to his garden,
To the beds of spices,
To feed in the gardens,
And to gather lilies.
I am my beloved's, and my beloved is mine,
That feedeth among the lilies.'

94

Superheroes

A young, scholarly, rather diffident man, shy with women and seemingly a pushover, kills a great warrior in battle, then becomes the head of his nation. One of the first Jewish superheroes was David, the slayer of Goliath.

It can be persuasively argued that an even greater Jewish titan was Moses, also known as "the Deliverer." Against all odds, parading about in his early years as a nephew of Pharaoh and a possible rival to Raamses for the throne of Egypt, cast out into the wilderness to perish only to return to deliver his people from bondage, Moses, a stutterer, inspired the parting of the Red Sea and the Israelites' return to their land of milk and honey.

Judah Maccabbee defeated the Hellenic Syrians mounted on elephants with cunning, sharp spears, and relentless fury. A few centuries later, Simon Bar Kokhba, "son of the Star," led a comparable but failed revolt against Roman oppression, which, had it succeeded, would have surpassed the Maccabbean revolt remembered today at Hanukkah.

There have been others in history who gave Jews great reason for pride in their superbly heroic deeds. Yet in more recent years there have seemed to be many more. Above all, the Warsaw Ghetto Uprising, led by twenty-four-year-old Mordecai Anielewicz, and the War of Israeli Independence have provided Jews with the greatest pride.

An interesting footnote to this history can be found in comic books. Most of the great superheroes such as that curiously Hebraic sounding alien, Kal-El, or Superman; Batman and Robin; Spiderman; and the Incredible Hulk were all created by Jewish writers and illustrators. Perhaps with the liberating force of American democracy surrounding them, Jews felt free to create superheroes out of their religious tradition for everyone to share and learn from their flights of courage.

95

Tikkun

Many scientists today believe the universe was created in a "big bang." The big bang theory, as it is called, may indeed have been reality, as scientists are beginning to find corroborating evidence for it in the void of the cosmos.

Lurianic Kabbalah is the name for the school of mysticism founded by the sage Isaac Luria in Safed during the sixteenth century. Luria was the leader of a small group of mystics who believed, in essence, in unique visions about the Creation. For Luria, the Creation began when the Divine Spirit contracted into itself (*tzimtzum* in Hebrew), releasing godly rays of light into the void. As these emanations went forth, a degradation occurred, a shattering of their pure shape. This "breaking of the vessels," or *shevirah*, is the metaphor used by Luria to describe the splintering of God's holy light. Something inherently bad hung onto the light, could not survive, except if it fed on the good. That something, what we call "evil," is the work of Satan and his followers. The light of God released from the holy vessels is rushing back to God. It is our responsibility to halt and bring it back into the world and prevent evil from consuming all existence.

Every Jew is responsible for putting these broken shards (*tikkun*) back together. Only when the vessels hold this holy light and the catastrophe is rectified will there be heaven on Earth.

Lurianic Kabbalah is a revolutionary creed. Yet it has been applied by the Orthodox as the spiritual core of religious worship. The redemption of the world through the acts of the Jewish people can occur only through strict adherence to Judaism's *halakhot*, or laws. By obeying halakhot in ritual and everyday living, belief in tikkun guarantees a path through righteous behavior to the healing of the world.

Tikkun is not just an abstract religious or mystical belief. It is a requirement. Tikkun is why we are all here. Every person has a responsibility to be virtuous—in *everything*—not an easy task in a world of ready answers and instant gratification. If we are not conscious of our joint and several responsibility, the light will go out of the world.

Tikkun is civilization.

96

Torah (As Story)

The greatest stories ever told are in the Torah.

Commentators and authors continue to discover in Genesis, for example, its relevance today. The powerful accounts of family life among the Patriarchs set forth in Genesis are timeless. Universal themes abound—brotherhood (Cain and Abel), reverence (Noah), monotheism (Abraham), infertility (Sarah), jealousy (Joseph and his brothers), obedience to God's laws and will (Moses). Helping the poor, sheltering the weak, looking after the widow, being responsible for each other, observing the Sabbath and keeping it holy, accepting God's direction over our lives, and ethical behavior are a few of the eternal strains in the Torah that will always be there to help make our discordant lives harmonious.

The Torah is the greatest bestselling book in history. So much so that the Christians and Muslims have their own versions! The Torah has proven highly adaptable to other cultures and religions. The tale of

the wanderings and transformation of Moses from prince, slave, Midian shepherd, to lawgiver is mirrored in the paths to righteousness of Jesus of Nazareth and the journey and ascension of the Prophet Muhammad.

The Torah contains the most compelling stories of any book. There is really nothing quite like it. It is impossible to name any other book that even comes close. All the archetypes found in literature today—*all*—were first set forth in the Torah. Of course, there is nothing new under the sun not first found in the Torah. The basic elements of character, plot line, literary devices, narrative, prose, poetry, history, fiction, and fantasy were initially expounded in the Torah. How people grow up; stay together as a family and a nation; love, hate, procreate, sing, kill, write, play, grow old, gain wisdom, go mad, die, and get born; Torah stories breathe with life.

97

Tradition

When Tevye (the milkman in Sholem Aleichem's stories and the hero of the musical *Fiddler on the Roof*) sang of tradition, he was thinking of *semikhah*.

Jewish tradition began when Moses in a gesture called "the laying on of hands," or semikhah, passed the Torah over to Joshua. Each succeeding generation has had the authority derived from Moses, the lawgiver, to pass on to the next the essentials of Judaism.

This ordination has resulted in an unbroken line of thinking and writing. Judaism's great strength is as a religion not only of belief but also of ideas, a "how to" faith adaptable to any age. Jews have never been afraid to ask "why." Their heritage encourages—in the context of Torah—reflection and inquiry. The respect for the Oral Law in Jewish tradition over the centuries has likewise insured that a "fence around the Torah" shields the religion from dilution and attack.

Some aspects of Jewish tradition have their origins in Jewish culture. The rabbis have accorded such traditional behavior and practices equality with custom grounded in Mosaic law. For example, Orthodox Jewry today views certain modes of dress as traditionally required and connoting a sacred purpose. Traditional dress, like customary chants in the synagogue, fosters an inevitability to life. To many observant Jews, this regularity and obedience to the past sets them free.

98

Tzedakah

The adage "It is better to give than receive" is so often quoted in our society. Perhaps it masks a pervasive guilt that taking seems more desirable than bestowing. There are so many charities today competing for our hard-earned money. At best, we can only respond to a few, covering our ears and closing our hearts and pocketbooks to most.

Yet charity can be extended without paying any money. Monetary donations can be supplemented or replaced by gifts of goods or services. Acts of loving-kindness can take many forms. Jewish law and custom requires that we be creative in seeking out such acts in everything we do. Also, the way we give, our care not to hurt the feelings or sensibilities of the recipient, marks us as civilized people.

Whether it be required by the Torah, commentary, rabbinical decree, or tradition, Judaism asks that one-tenth of a person's holdings and consequent earnings be given away to those less fortunate. The giver is warned, however, not to contribute more than 20 percent as he, himself, might then need aid.

Jewish regard for those less fortunate goes back to Biblical times. "Alms for the poor" shrieked by a tattered beggar is a widely held image of the ancient world for many (mostly from films). And, this impression is not far from the truth. The divide between the well-to-do and the poor was much wider then than it is now, and even today the epidemic of poverty still overwhelms and leaves us unable to cope successfully with its numbing enormity.

Jews created some of the earliest examples of charitable organizations. Every community was urged to consolidate its efforts by forming groups committed to helping the needy. Jewish charities today compete with each other to provide social and medical services to those less fortunate in innovative programs and with a holy zeal in outdoing each other.

Maimonides recognized eight ascending degrees of giving, starting with resenting the person to whom you are giving to making that person self-sufficient. The debates today about the American welfare system focus on these same issues that Maimonides recognized over a thousand years ago. The Jewish way of giving has helped provide a civilized example for all the world to emulate.

Charity in Hebrew is the widely known word *tzedakah*. Young Hebrew school students are instructed to throw something in the collection box. It is a lesson well taught, for the roots of tzedakah are in justice. Through giving, we redeem the world.

99

Tzaddikim

The Babylonian Talmud relates that if there are not thirty-six righteous men alive at any one time, then the world will surely perish. The Hebrew word for righteous men is *tzaddikim*.

Tradition holds that the tzaddik goes about doing his good deeds quietly. No one knows of his special view of life. The tzaddik values only what can be done for others. Charitable acts, denying one's own needs for others, are the signs of the righteous. Tzaddikim do not know of each other's existence. They are visible when Jews are in trouble only to vanish when the trouble ends.

Orthodox groups such as the Hasidim view their leader, usually called the rebbe, as a tzaddik. His every word is listened to, since he is considered to be as God's direct representative and visionary on earth.

The importance of the concept of the tzaddikim is that the major reason for our lives is to assist other people. Tzaddikim are filled with *shekhinah*, God's presence, or spirit. A world ready to be destroyed is one in which the essence of God's giving is absent. One of the great contributions of Judaism to the world in which Jews can find great satisfaction is the notion that doing for others is the reward for our lives.

100

Yiddish

To misstate a hackneyed expression, the death of Yiddish has been widely reported for years.

Prior to the Shoah, there were eleven million Yiddish-speaking people in the world. Mass murder and assimilation have severely reduced that number. Yet the language survives today, particularly in yeshivot and among the ultra-Orthodox in America and Israel. Although many Jews cannot speak Yiddish fluently, most know at least a handful of words that they use repeatedly.

Since the early Middle Ages until the post–World War II period, Yiddish served as the lingua franca between Jews of differing towns or nations. Despite its use in "high" literature and drama, Yiddish was always a language of everyman. The rich could speak it to the poor, Jews from Romania could converse with their brethren in Poland, esteemed rabbinical sages used it to communicate with uneducated common folk. Merchants could venture forth over long distances with a mother tongue that summed up in pithy and often richly personal expressions just what one needed to say. Many who spoke Yiddish knew no Hebrew other than prayers.

The word *Yiddish* was created as a shortening of *yiddish daytsch*, or German Yiddish. Yiddish is an amalgam of medieval Rhenish German and Hebrew characters (as well as sprinklings of the languages of the countries in which Jews made their homes before 1940). Phrases derived from life, intimate sayings not easily translatable into other tongues, sharp and direct utterances seemingly from the gut—all constituted a language unlike any other.

Before the establishment of the State of Israel, Hebrew was considered by most Ashkenazim as too sacred to use in everyday speech. Yiddish could be used for everything, freely, without the risk of profaning some holy scripture or hallowed thought.

Yiddish curses and vulgarity (for example, "May all your teeth fall out except one, and may that hurt!" or "When the penis stands up, the brains are in the earth!") are unique and irreplaceable, capable of going straight to the heart, punching one verbally in the stomach, or lifting one's feet into the clouds. In Yiddish everyone had their say, from the most cultured aesthete to the rabbi teaching cheder (religious school) to the mama rocking her *totele* (little boy) to sleep. Yiddish inspired poets, novelists, historians, and playwrights to create a vast and profound body of literature.

Yiddish was the foundation of Ashkenazic civilization.

101

Yiddish Theater

When my father was five years old, he sold drinks and candy to a Yiddish-speaking audience in the Liberty Theater, in Brownsville, Brooklyn.

In 1923 (Sam Shapiro was five), New York City had a vibrant Yiddish theater that had developed along with the large influx of Eastern European Jews. It was largely centered around Second Avenue below 14th Street (although there were other areas in New York City that boasted of Yiddish productions such as the Liberty Theater in Brooklyn). The Second Avenue Yiddish theater would last only another forty years or so. In Poland, as well, from the late 1800s through as late as 1968, Yiddish theater flourished in Warsaw and Cracow, reaching its apogee in the classic performances of Ida Kaminska. In Russia, Yiddish theater only prospered during brief periods when the Communists eased their control. Except for nostalgic productions in the United States and occasional revivals in Israel, the Yiddish stage is largely silent today. Unlike klezmer music, which is undergoing a revival and is still being composed (music needs no translator), there are few, if any, new significant Yiddish plays.

The history of Yiddish theater is therefore brief. There were no Yiddish playwrights at the Globe Theatre during Elizabethan times, none during the reign of Louis XIV at Versailles, nor at Ford's Theater just after the Civil War. Yiddish theater only thrived when Jews were allowed by civil authorities to congregate—*in a secular place*. In the Diaspora, when Jews massed together, it was always to pray, not to be entertained. Jews came together largely for religious reasons or for ancillary gatherings such as circumcisions, weddings, and funerals.

But with their first taste of freedom (especially in America), they sought entertainment. The Yiddish theater provided a glimpse of a life denied to immigrants in their native lands. Many of the Yiddish plays looked back to the shtetl. Some were based on Sholem Aleichem's tales or on wild visions of golems and dybbuks. Others attempted to help greenhorn cousins from the Old Country learn about America. Classics were also translated; Hamlet's soliloquy "To be or not to be" was passionately declaimed in Yiddish by Maurice Schwartz. Culture was imported from Merrie Olde Englande through Mein Shtetele Belz to East 4th Street.

Without a fluent Yiddish-speaking audience and faced with a largely assimilated public attracted mostly to popular American entertainment, a profit-making Yiddish theater faded into history. Yet it is a sign of Yiddish pride that when Jews found freedom they also proudly discovered their dramatic voice.

Acknowledgments

First and foremost, my love to my wife, Theresa, for her immeasurable support during an arduous task. She is—and has always been—my inspiration, my kindest and best friend.

To friends and colleagues: the entire Angelus family, Diane Behar, Ed and Tracy Berkman, Jessica Black, Edward Brown, Peter and Myra Cole, Jan Colijn, Ion and Merope Collas, John Corigliano, Nicholas and Nancy D'Agostino, Barry and Janet Davis, Faye DiRosa, Harold and Nina Fetner, Molly Friedrich, Sharon Gutman and Charles Lightner, Jonathan Heine, William M. Hoffman, Dr. Helene Kaminski, James and Peter Kempner, Florence Levitt, Franklin Levy, Marcia Sachs Littell and Franklin Littell, Areti and Ourania Lolis, Mark Ludwig, Natalie Manzino, Allan and Bitsy Maraynes, Todd and Nan Mason, Lawrence Mass, John Mauceri, Maggie McComas and Henry Muller, Victor Menkin, Andrew and Edith Mermell, John Edward Niles, Yehuda Nir, Abraham and Jean Peck, Sander and Mechele Flaum, Harris and LaVonne Poor, Kevin and Consuelo Prol, Gil Robinov, Jerome Rose, Stewart and Mindy Rosenblatt, Camille Saviola, Jim and Ann Shankman, Stewart and Judy Simon, Richard and Dianne Spitalny, Teresa Stratas, Gottfried and Teresina Wagner, and John Waxman, grateful thanks for your ideas and enthusiasm.

Special appreciation goes to David Harris, executive director of the American Jewish Committee, and Dr. Marvin Chinitz for their useful suggestions and clarifications. Without the skillful attention of physical therapist Dorothy Pawlowski and ophthalmologist Dr. Nan Hayworth, my back and eyes would not have made it through the first draft.

My friend and publisher, Steven Schragis, was with me when the idea for this book was first enunciated. Allan Wilson, my editor, provided encouragement and was graciously attentive to a harried author.

My wonderful family was again there to help show me the way. Cousin Noah Millman was especially helpful in organizing and thinking through with me the concepts set out in this book, and his father, Dr. Arthur Millman, also provided many of the texts used in valuable research. My dear siblings-in-law Marjorie, Catherine, Carl, and Tina, my mother-in-law, Mary Vorgia, and cousins Laura, Felella, Carolyn, and Ilana, were also supportive and kind to me during a particularly stressful time. I am so proud of my parents, Sam and Jean Shapiro, my favorite aunt, Jean, my artistic cousin, John Morrin, and my brother Barry for their humane leadership in our proud Jewish family. Jewish pride certainly does start at home with family and friends.

About the Author

MICHAEL SHAPIRO is the author of the bestselling *The Jewish 100: A Ranking of the Most Influential Jews of All Time.* He is a partner in the New York law firm of Shereff, Friedman, Hoffman and Goodman L.L.P. Mr. Shapiro is active in New York's Jewish community, including involvement with the American Jewish Committee and the Post-Holocaust Dialogue Group. He is a noted composer of more than a hundred works including operatic, symphonic, choral, chamber, and solo pieces and has served as a music consultant to the United States Holocaust Memorial Museum. Many of his compositions are based on Jewish subjects.